# *African Americans*
## OF
## ST. LAWRENCE COUNTY

# *African Americans*

## OF

## ST. LAWRENCE COUNTY

### NORTH COUNTRY PIONEERS

BRYAN S. THOMPSON

THE
History
PRESS

Published by The History Press
Charleston, SC
www.historypress.com

*Front cover, top right*: Courtesy of the *Aluminum Bulletin* at St. Lawrence County Historical Association Archives.

First published 2023

Manufactured in the United States

ISBN 9781467154031

Library of Congress Control Number: 2023937168

*For Julia and Isaac*
*Not the first. Not the last. Part of a never-ending stream.*

# CONTENTS

# FOREWORD

I n *African Americans of St. Lawrence County*, Bryan Thompson turns upside
down the idea that African Americans were, until recently, absent
from St. Lawrence County in New York State. As he convincingly
shows, African Americans have had a continuous presence in this northern
county since the mid-eighteenth century and have contributed to shaping
it into a diverse community. Some African Americans there were enslaved,
but others were activist abolitionists and spiritual leaders or property and
business owners. The scarcity of African Americans in the county by the
1930s was the result of intentional exclusion by economic and legal barriers
and by racism.

Thompson has been immersed in the history of New York's North
Country for his entire life. His writing ties local history to the largest
themes in national and international history: slavery, wars, reform and
racist movements. He details this local history by making use of myriad
types of historical sources: legal documents; census records; African
American, local and national newspapers; business records; oral histories;
and correspondence. As a dedicated rural historian, he can decipher
documents and also read a landscape. He will happily travel to a distant
archive to do research on his community. But for him, a tramp through
a nearby woods offers as good an opportunity to understand human
exchanges and their impact on the natural world.

Thompson is also a teacher who has shared his historical passions with
all ages in the classroom and in public forums for decades. For the last

sixteen years, he has served as New York State's Town of De Kalb historian and archivist, garnering awards for education, preservation, research and writing. He has shared much of this work in the *Williamstown Gazette*, which he has published since 1996.

Bryan Thompson has never been content to focus only on those aspects of community life that encourage ancestral pride. His research encourages a deeper understanding of our inheritance by including people and structures invisible in existing histories. His diligent methodology as well as his absorbing narrative are gifts to us all.

—M.J. Heisey
Professor emeritus
Department of History
State University of New York at Potsdam
January 2023

# ACKNOWLEDGEMENTS

There are so many people who have encouraged and helped me along the way. I especially want to thank my neighbor and friend Dr. M.J. Heisey and Dr. Melissane Schrems for reviewing various drafts of this book and providing me with valuable feedback. I would like to also acknowledge Neil Burdick for his editorial assistance.

Don Papson has always had an ear for me and sent me in the right direction for research, especially early in this project. Betsy Kepes was always ready to read drafts and provide feedback throughout the project.

I thank the staff of the St. Lawrence County Law Library for their assistance in researching the various laws. I would like to also acknowledge the ready assistance of the St. Lawrence County Historical Association and the Potsdam Museum. Thanks to Greg Hyde for providing me with space to retreat and write so many times. Thanks to all my other friends—Raymond, Susan, Claude, Tom, John, Karen, Valerie and all the rest—for supporting me during the process.

I want to acknowledge my elementary school teacher Marion Sheen for discussing the civil rights movement with us on a weekly basis, as it happened, and teaching us that no matter who we are, we all bleed red. I must thank my grandmother Adeline Thompson for first putting the "story" in history for me. And last but not least, I want to thank my husband, Gary Berk, for putting up with me over the many years it has taken to research and write this book.

# INTRODUCTION

I grew up on a typical family farm in St. Lawrence County, New York, during the 1960s. We milked forty cows, made maple syrup and sold a few other commodities from the farm. We lived near Beaver Creek just a few miles from where my ancestors (Sweet, Hurlbut, Giffin) had settled seven generations before. My world was totally white and seemed to have always been that way. However, as I learned in the course of researching this book, that was a myth.

Every story has its beginning. For this book, it was at a fourth-grade parent-teacher conference for my adopted Black son. I asked the teacher what Black history my child had learned during the year. The teacher's response was, "Your son was sick the day we talked about Black history."

I kept my cool at the meeting, but I was flabbergasted. You mean the whole Black experience in New York State and local history over three hundred years warranted only one day? (Having taught elementary social studies methods at SUNY Potsdam, I knew what the curriculum was supposed to include.) Weren't there Black people present throughout every day of our history? Surely every child, including my son, deserved to see their race, ethnicity, gender and sexuality reflected in the history of their community on a daily basis in the same way white children do.

And so I began to dig into local records. That's when I came across Charlie Clark, a Black man who had lived for a time on the very farm where I had grown up only sixty-five years before. Why had no one ever mentioned him to me?

I looked for articles and books detailing the stories of our St. Lawrence County Black community. The stories were almost nonexistent. As a seventh-generation St. Lawrence County resident and a local historian, I felt compelled to find the hidden histories of our Black pioneers.

As I began to research, I discovered that there were Black people present in the county from the very first incursions of the non-aboriginal people into the area. These people were essential to the success of these early settlement activities. Some became famous in their own right; some served this country in its time of need and remained totally unrecognized. These people are an important part of the history of St. Lawrence County, New York State and the United States. Removing their history from our collective memory does us all a disservice.

I began this book so that every teacher of history would have some background in local Black history. As I researched and wrote, it quickly became apparent that the contributions of African Americans to St. Lawrence County history were not separate from the state, national and international stage but an integral part of it. The audience for this book is much broader than I originally imagined. It reaches from teachers, public historians and professional scholars to university students and fans of American history. I hope that this work will inspire others to continue this important research, because I have only scratched the surface.

## CHAPTER 1

# NEW FRANCE (1749–1760) AND BRITISH NORTH AMERICA (1763–1797)

## NEW FRANCE

When commencing a story, it is best to begin at the beginning. For the Black pioneers of the St. Lawrence River Valley, that is at the start of the incursion of non-Indigenous people into the area. Although the sources I have on New France provide only brief glimpses of life, even in those snapshots, Black people are present. We cannot have an accurate history of St. Lawrence County without acknowledging their presence and contributions. Other researchers with access to other sources will undoubtedly build on this chapter's documentation of Black pioneers who appear in sources I combed with this important focus at the forefront.

The French had already been in the St. Lawrence Valley for over a century when they finally established a settlement in 1749 at la Présentation (today's Ogdensburg, New York). La Preséntation was the last of a string of Catholic mission communities founded along the St. Lawrence known as the "Seven Nations" or "Seven Castles" with governance patterned after the Haudenosaunee Confederacy.

The first Black slave was brought to New France by the British commander David Kirk in 1628. This Black man, Olivier Le Juene, native of Madagascar, died in 1654. There were, however, very few slaves in New France until the end of the seventeenth century. Most were brought to the colony by traveling merchants from neighboring British colonies or were Indigenous slaves (*Panis*)[1] given as tokens of respect to the French overlords by Indigenous people. In fact, two-thirds of the slaves in New France were Panis.

The institution of slavery was legalized in New France by Intendant Jacques Raudot on April 13, 1709, with the following order: "All Panis and Negroes who have been purchased and who will be purchased, shall be the property of those who have purchased them and will be their slaves. It shall be forbidden to said Panis and Negroes to leave their masters, and whosoever shall incite them to leave their masters shall be subjected to a fine of fifty pounds."[2]

The number of slaves in New France grew astronomically following the issue of this edict. However, ownership of slaves was limited to the elite of Quebec society. Colonial governors, intendants (who oversaw civil administration), clergy, religious communities, military officers, merchants and traders were the most common masters. Two-thirds of all slave owners in New France owned only one slave. Black slaves cost twice as much as Indigenous slaves and usually lived in the homes of their masters.

La Présentation was founded in May 1749 by a French party led by Abbé Picquet. Regular colonial correspondence seldom mentioned slaves. It is only by chance that when Abbé Piquet was returning to France in August

Fort la Présentation. *From* A History of St. Lawrence and Franklin Counties New York from the Earliest Period to the Present Time *(Albany, NY: Franklin Hough, 1853)*.

1753 to visit the court of Louis XV, we learn of his ownership of "Charles negro slave of M. Picquet"[3] on the roster of passengers of the king's ship *l'Algonkin* sailing for Brest.

Piquet first sailed to the Quebec district of New France in 1733. For about seven years, he worked in Montreal. In about 1740, he established himself at the Sulpician Order mission at Lake of Two Mountains (Oka). There were a number of slaves owned by the community. This is most likely when Abbé Piquet came into possession of Charles.

It is likely that Charles accompanied Piquet on his numerous forays into the interior of the country along the St. Lawrence River and around the Great Lakes. As a personal servant, Charles would have been responsible for the daily care of Piquet's personal needs. He would have helped to pitch camp, forage for food, keep fires, wash and prepare vestments and perform any other tasks assigned to him by his master.

When Piquet founded la Présentation, there was a severe shortage of labor. Garrisoned French soldiers refused to do any manual labor. It fell to the civilians who were Indigenous Oswegatchie,[4] *habitants* (French colonial settlers) and, of course, the slaves to clear the land and build the settlement. Piquet was quite successful in his endeavor. In just three years, the settlement included Fort la Présentation, a sawmill that provided sawn lumber for all the French outposts on Lake Ontario, about one hundred acres of cleared land with many acres of Indian corn and about forty-nine traditional longhouses, which housed up to three thousand Oswegatchie.

Charles was not the only Black person in the community. Burial records for an Oswegatchie baby privately baptized say the midwife was a "negress." So there was at least one Black woman in the community performing the essential service of midwifery to the Oswegatchie.

When Abbé Piquet returned from his trip to the French court in May 1754, he brought with him two fellow members of his Sulpician Order. One of these priests, Pierre-Paul-François de Lagarde, came to la Présentation immediately after he was ordained in Quebec City in May 1755. He was accompanied by his slave, Anselme, who had been baptized in 1749. Anselme would have been present through all of the military maneuvers at la Présentation in the last five years of its existence. His master Abbé Lagarde remained at the French settlement after Abbé Piquet fled. Lagarde was taken prisoner at the capitulation of Fort Levis in August 1760. Abbé Lagarde was paroled along with two or three soldiers' wives and given permission to return to Montreal. Presumably, Anselme was by his side through all these events. Anselme died at the Hospital General in Montreal that same year and was buried on the hospital grounds.[5]

We may have yet another Black man, who appears in the writing of Robert Eastburn, a tradesman. Eastburn was caught up in the Fort Bull Campaign in March 1756. He was one of the party of settlers captured by the Oswegatchie near Fort William (Oneida County). Unlike those who were at Fort Bull, this party was not massacred. They were taken prisoner and force-marched back to la Présentation. In Eastburn's published account, he relates many events while he was a prisoner in New France. Eventually, he was adopted into a native Oswegatchie family at la Présentation.[6]

During the time Eastburn was at la Présentation, Abbé Piquet determined to refortify the town by digging a large trench around it. The construction of the moat was managed by a Black man who could speak English, French and "Indian" (perhaps an Iroquoian language) fluently.[7] Eastburn was paid in board and most importantly in cash, which he needed for an unsuccessful

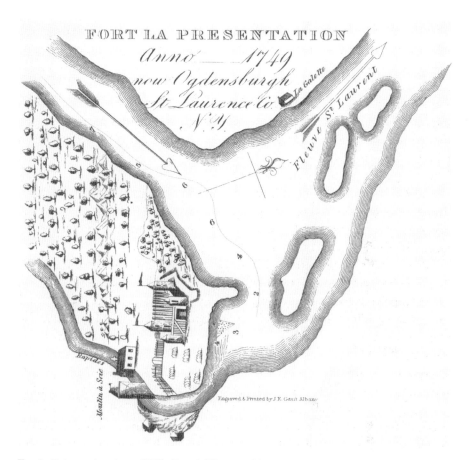

Fort la Présentation Anno 1749. *From* A History of St. Lawrence and Franklin Counties New York from the Earliest Period to the Present Time *(Albany, NY: Franklin Hough, 1853).*

escape attempt. Here we have another glimpse of a Black person, fluent in three languages, living at la Présentation, serving in the role of foreman or engineer in charge of building extra fortifications.

La Présentation, the first European-controlled settlement in St. Lawrence County, was a diverse, multi-ethnic community. The settlement was supervised by French clergy who demanded sobriety and industriousness of its residents. The inhabitants were largely Oswegatchies from many Indigenous communities but also included French habitants, Germans, English, French soldiers and several Black people. At least five languages are documented as being spoken in the community. Three thousand people of diverse backgrounds lived contentedly side by side at its peak in the 1750s.

# BRITISH NORTH AMERICA

Little has been written about the history of St. Lawrence County in the period from the end of the Seven Years' War to the British evacuation of Fort Oswegatchie in 1796. Even the date of the evacuation when the county became part of the fledgling United States is unknown today. We know that Edward Darcy attempted to establish a settlement in 1774 near Black Lake, known as Darcyville, and developed an eel weir downstream on the Oswegatchie River. Today, all that is left of this venture is Lost Village Road in the town of Oswegatchie.

However, from the end of the Seven Years' War—also known, primarily in North America, as the French and Indian War—until the signing of the Jay Treaty, there was much activity among the local Indigenous population. Many of the former inhabitants of la Présentation moved east to Indian Point on the St. Lawrence River (now the old state hospital grounds), where they established a European worker-style village, only to be evicted in 1806. One famous person of Black ancestry came to dwell in the county during this period: Louis Atiatoharongwan Cook.

In 1745, a raiding party from the Seven Nations community of Kahnawa:ke, Quebec, descended on the frontier community of Fort Saratoga (Schuylerville). As part of the spoils of war, they captured a group of African slaves, one of whom was married to an Abenaki woman, Molly Montour. The party's intention was to sell all of the slaves. Molly Montour had a young son, Nia-man-rigounant, half Black, among those who were about to be sold. She protested and was allowed to keep her son, who would become famous as Louis Atiatoharongwan Cook.

The pair were taken to Kahnawa:ke, Quebec, where they were adopted into the community. Young Louis was a quick learner. Converting to Catholicism, he soon mastered French and Mohawk to add to his knowledge of English and Abenaki. Louis became a loyal supporter of his adopted land. As a young warrior, he fought alongside the French in the Seven Years' War. He developed a lifelong animosity toward the British as a result and a few years later led the Mohawk faction, which sided with the colonists during the American Revolution. After the Seven Years' War, Cook returned to Kahnawa:ke, where he married Marie Charlotte.

At the outbreak of the American Revolution in 1775, Louis Cook marched south from Kahnawa:ke with his supporters. They met up with General Washington and Schuyler near Albany. Always a politician, Cook exaggerated the support for the Revolution among the Seven Nations. He

Colonel Louis Cook. Sketch by John Trumbull, 1785. *Yale University Art Museum.*

was commissioned as a lieutenant colonel in the Continental army. The only Black man to serve as an officer in the ranks, he became known as "Colonel Louis" and was a great asset to Washington's army. The Continental Congress made his commission official on June 15, 1779, and renewed it until the end of the war in July 1782.

Colonel Cook saw action at the Battle of Oriskany in the Saratoga Campaign. He marched on Quebec City, was a hero of the Battle of Klock's Field and was present at Valley Forge. In March 1778, he marched to the

Niagara Frontier to destroy British ships. He was present at the Battle of Johnstown. In 1780, Colonel Cook was sent to present a native delegation to the French General Rochambeau. It was noted by an officer in attendance that Cook spoke fluent French without any trace of an accent.

The Revolution had a devastating effect on the Haudenosaunee, who had fought on both sides. After the war, Louis Cook first settled among the Oneidas, where he married his second wife, Marguerite Thewanihattha. She was a daughter of a notable Oneida leader, Skenandoa.

Louis Cook was a notoriously mercurial politician. He became too involved in Oneida tribal politics and land negotiations. In 1789, a group of Oneidas complained to New York governor George Clinton that Louis had attempted to enslave them. Louis soon removed north with most of his family to the area that would eventually become the St. Lawrence County town of Massena. The area had been the territory of the Akwesasne since 1754. His son Logan or Loran would remain behind on his old lands on Oneida Creek near Sterling Road.

In 1790, the United States passed the Non-Intercourse Act, which gave the federal government sole power to negotiate with Native nations. Over the next decade, New York State would ignore the federal law and on its own negotiate several treaties with various factions of the St. Regis Mohawks and the Kahnawa:ke (Seven Nations).

Colonel Louis Cook with his command of languages was a favorite negotiator with New York for the Kahnawa:ke. By 1796, he had successfully negotiated a treaty with New York State that expanded the lands held by the Mohawks at Akwesasne. The new lands included a mile square (six hundred acres) on the Grasse River where the village of Massena is today and the nearby meadows on the Grasse River to its mouth. Also included was a mile square east of the original reservation in what would become the town of Fort Covington. This treaty led to more infighting among the various Mohawk factions.

Colonel Cook took up residence on the square mile where Massena village stands today. He erected several mills on the Grasse River and established a settlement there. Cook continued to live in the town of Massena until the War of 1812 broke out. By this time, Cook was in his late seventies. Seizing the opportunity to stand against his nemesis the British and support his American allies, Cook traveled to Plattsburgh, Sacketts Harbor and the Niagara Frontier with his sons to offer his services.

British colonel De Lorimer sent word ahead of Cook's arrival at Niagara that Cook was a double agent not to be trusted. Colonel Cook was locked up in the stockade for eight days upon his arrival. During questioning, Cook presented his pocket book containing his commission, General Washington's letter of commendation and several other letters of commendation from prominent military men.

Colonel Cook was released and allowed to accompany General Brown's troops into Canada commanding a detachment of Six Nations warriors. He saw action at the Battles of Chippewa and Lundy's Lane in Canada. After the campaign, he became seriously ill. He died at a Haudenosaunee village near Buffalo, New York, in October 1814. He was buried there with full military honors.

Although Cook lived the lifestyle of his adopted Mohawk brothers, the British and Americans never ceased pointing out his African heritage whenever it was to their advantage, referring to him as "African Louis," "Black Louis" and "the half-negro from Canada."

## TIMELINE, CHAPTER 1

| | |
|---|---|
| 1605 | Samuel de Champlain establishes Fort Royal, first successful French settlement. |
| 1607 May | Jamestown founded as first British settlement in North America. |
| 1608 June | Champlain leads settlement of Quebec City, founding New France. |
| 1619 | First Black enslaved people arrive in Virginia colony. |
| 1620 December | Plymouth colony founded. |
| 1624 | Dutch establish first permanent settlement at Fort Orange (Albany, New York). |
| 1626 | First enslaved Black men brought to New Netherlands. |
| 1628 | Olivier Le Juene, first Black slave, brought to New France. |

| | |
|---|---|
| 1709 April 13 | Institution of slavery in New France legalized. |
| 1740 | Louis Atiatoharongwan Cook born, Schuylerville, New York. |
| 1745 | Kahnawa:ke raiding party capture Louis Atiatoharongwan Cook and his mother near Fort Saratoga. |
| 1749 May | La Présentation founded by Abbé Piquet accompanied by his enslaved servant Charles, first known Black person in St. Lawrence County. |
| 1753 August | Abbé Piquet sails for France to visit the court of Louis XIV, accompanied by Charles. |
| 1754 | Abbe Pierre-Paul-François de Lagarde arrives at La Présentation accompanied by Anselme, an enslaved Black man. |
| 1759 September | Fort Levis constructed on Isle Royale. |
| 1760 August 25 | Abbe Pierre-Paul-François de Lagarde and Anselme are present at the Battle of Fort Levis. |
| 1760 | Anselme dies at the hospital in Montreal and is buried there. |
| 1760 September 8 | Marquis de Vaudreil signs articles of capitulation of Montreal, completing British conquest of New France. |
| 1763 February 10 | Treaty of Paris officially ends French and Indian War. |
| 1775 | Louis Atiatoharongwan Cook marches south to near Albany, where he forms an alliance with American revolutionaries. He is commissioned a lieutenant colonel. |
| 1779 June 15 | Continental Congress makes Louis Atiatoharongwan Cook's commission official. |
| 1792 | Louis Atiatoharongwan Cook arrives at Akwesasne. |

| | |
|---|---|
| 1796 February 29 | Jay Treaty goes into effect. |
| 1796 | British evacuate Fort Oswegatchie at Ogdensburg. St. Lawrence County officially becomes part of the United States. |
| 1812 | War with Britain declared, officially starting War of 1812. |
| 1814 July 5 | Louis Atiatoharongwan Cook leads group of Iroquois soldiers in the Battle of Chippewa. |
| 1814 July 25 | Cook leads group of Iroquois soldiers in the Battle of Lundy's Lane. |
| 1814 October | Cook dies in Native village outside Buffalo. |

CHAPTER 2

# THE SLAVE YEARS (1797–1827)

W hile sources on New France are limited, sources on Black Americans in the late eighteenth- and early nineteenth-century colonial and early U.S. national periods provide more detailed pictures of Black pioneers in St. Lawrence County. The myth has been perpetuated for many generations that enslaved people were few and far between and were treated more benevolently in the North than in the South. In fact, slavery was an everyday part of life in the northern colonies prior to the American Revolution. The first enslaved people were imported to New York in 1626, Massachusetts in 1624, Connecticut in 1639, New Hampshire in 1645 and Rhode Island in 1652. By the middle of the eighteenth century, Newport, Rhode Island, hosted the largest slave auction in the colonies.

For the first settlers of St. Lawrence County, slavery was a fact of life. Slavery had been present in New York for generations. Slavery was so common that almost everyone had firsthand knowledge of it. (To say otherwise would be akin to claiming that a twenty-first-century St. Lawrence County resident did not know what a large-screen TV was. You may not own one yourself, but you surely have seen one and know what it is.)

In the state of New York at the time of the American Revolution, there were more enslaved people than in any of the other northern states in the newly founded republic. At the first New York State constitutional convention in 1777, Gouverneur Morris, soon to be proprietor of the St. Lawrence County towns of Gouverneur and Morristown, introduced a resolution to ban slavery. The motion failed.

In 1788, the New York state legislature passed an act banning the slave trade in the state. The bill, however, did not ban the indenturing of servants even up to ninety-nine years. Slavery did not disappear. Children born to an enslaved mother were still the property of their mother's master. Most sales of enslaved people, however, were listed as indentures. In fact, New York State's colonial slave codes remained in effect until the end of slavery in the state, which happened only gradually.

As described by historian Ira Berlin in *Many Thousands Gone*, New York and the other northern states were societies with slaves rather than slave societies.[8] In most cases, households owned just one or two enslaved people, who were housed with the owner's family but usually in an attic or cellar. Very few of New York's enslaved were allowed to live in their own households or to raise families. In addition, enslaved people were not allowed to form churches or other community organizations. Population decline was a continual problem for owners of enslaved people in the state. The number-one cause of death among enslaved people in New York was suicide.

In 1799, the New York state legislature passed Chapter 62 of the Laws of New York, "An Act for the Gradual Abolition of Slavery." The act freed all children born to enslaved mothers after July 4, 1799. Male children would not be freed until the age of twenty-eight and female children when they reached the age of twenty-five. This allowed owners of enslaved people to recoup economic losses by keeping these young enslaved individuals through their most productive years. Enslaved people born before July 4, 1799, were not freed so as to prevent masters from abandoning old or disabled enslaved people to local poor relief systems. The act required owners of enslaved people to record the births of all enslaved children. The bill also barred the sale of enslaved people outside the state.

New York State's Chapter 188 of the Laws of 1801 altered the 1799 act. The change allowed masters to free children at the age of one by signing them up as freed paupers with the overseer of the poor. The former owners would then be compensated by New York State at the rate of $3 per month for caring for the paupers (the 1799 law paid former owners $3.50 per month). This clause was so popular with owners of enslaved people that legislators had to amend the bill the next year (Chapter 52 of the Laws of 1802) to reduce the monthly payment to former owners to $2 per month and only until the child reached four years of age. Owners who signed up early were allowed to keep and use the labor of enslaved children while being compensated by the State of New York until they reached adulthood. The abandonment act became so expensive for the state that in 1804, it repealed that section of the law. The 1804 amendment also lowered the ages for the manumission of enslaved people to eighteen for females and twenty-one for males.[9]

The 1801 law stipulated that no enslaved person could testify in court against a white person. Furthermore, enslaved people were forbidden to mount any defense if accused of striking a white person. The accuser had only to give a sworn statement to have the enslaved person punished.

Under the 1801 law, all owners bringing enslaved people with them to live in New York had to file a certificate with their county clerk that they had owned the person for at least one year and that they would not sell the person outside the state. Failure to file such a document could lead to the emancipation of the enslaved person. David Ford filed such an oath with the St. Lawrence County clerk in December 1805, attesting to the fact that he had brought an eleven-year-old female enslaved person named Jude with him from Morris County, New Jersey, in June 1805. He also testified that he had owned her for at least a year before he arrived.[10]

In 1817, emancipation was extended to all enslaved people born before July 4, 1799. They were to be freed on July 4, 1827. However, the indenture clause for children of enslaved people remained intact, so many children remained in servitude until their twenty-first birthday. Although the statutory fine for selling enslaved people out of state was $250, owners were seldom prosecuted. Between 1810 and 1830, the Black population of the state diminished significantly.

The general picture of New York State's Black population, enslaved and free in rural areas, is enriched by portraits of individuals in St. Lawrence County evident in family papers, local histories and newspapers.

## THE HASBROUCK FAMILY ENSLAVED PEOPLE

Louis Hasbrouck was a member of the prestigious Hasbrouck family of Dutchess County. His father, Joseph Hasbrouck, had served as a lieutenant colonel during the Revolutionary War. Joseph owned thirteen enslaved people in 1790. By 1800, Louis owned four enslaved people. Louis entered the bar at Albany in 1801. He moved to Ogdensburg to serve as the first St. Lawrence County clerk in June 1802.[11] He continued to maintain a house in Ulster County and winter there at least until 1814. Louis Hasbrouck married Catherine Banks in December 1802. Catherine brought an enslaved woman, Nanny, to the marriage; Nanny had been raised with Catherine in Catherine's father's household.

When Hasbrouck moved his young family to Ogdensburg in 1804, they were accompanied by Nanny. The trip was a long and difficult one on primitive roads, dodging stumps and wallowing through mud holes and often reduced to traveling on foot, freezing in winter and bug-infested in summer.

Nanny performed many of the daily tasks to build and maintain a house in frontier Ogdensburg. These responsibilities included tending the eternal household fires, cooking, cleaning, washing, gardening and tending to her mistress in her laying in at childbirth.

Winters in civilized Ulster County must have been a relief. By the winter of 1810, Hasbrouck is listed on the census as owning three enslaved people in Ulster County.

Nanny was born into the household of Catherine Banks Hasbrouck's parents. Nanny's father was Jerry, a slave owned by Catherine's parents. As she was raised in the Banks household, Nanny may have felt like a member

Louis Hasbrouck's bill of sale for his enslaved person Nanny and her child. *Hasbrouck Family Papers, Ogdensburg Public Library Special Collections.*

of the family, but her masters considered her and all enslaved people "stock." This was made abundantly clear in a letter from Joseph Hasbrouck to his brother Louis in January 1812, regarding the division of their father's estate: "Phillip [their brother] took Dick, Har and Tobi along with him. I kept none of the old stock except Janet....When I got rid of the old stock I immediately went and purchased a black man, a woman and two children."[12]

Letters between Catherine Hasbrouck and her two sisters often contain little tidbits of news from Nanny's old enslaved friends and family. Eliza (Banks) Graham noted in August 1805: "Diana and Phillis says I must let Nanny know they have handsome new calico frocks."[13] Sarah (Banks) Lasher wrote in July 1809: "The kitchen folk are all well, Frances and York have made a visit lately of a fortnight and all send their love to Nanny."[14]

An additional note in Eliza Graham's letter reveals a much darker side to enslavement in New York State: "Pompey has had a mind to come in the chamber to see Miss Diana, but was found out and (he) looked like a squirrel that is treed running over the roof. (We went) after him in our chemise."[15] (Pompey and Diana were both slaves in the Graham household.)

All Black social organizations including churches were banned in the state after an early eighteenth-century slave uprising. No slave (such as Pompey) could marry without his master's consent. Most households had only one or two slaves, and it was considered a moral failing if one of the master's servants became pregnant. This led to a constantly decreasing Black population.

Nanny could not marry without the explicit permission of her masters. It must have been a lonely life for Nanny in the frontier village of Ogdensburg far from her Ulster County family and friends. However, this situation would change in early 1812 and would totally upend Nanny's life.

About this time, Nanny secretly found herself a paramour among the young men of Ogdensburg. As the year progressed, it became obvious that Nanny was pregnant, much to Catherine Hasbrouck's chagrin. The Hasbrouck family stayed in the village through the military build-up in the summer and early fall of 1812 despite the pleas of their extended family in Ulster County that they come back to Ulster.

Finally, after the failed attack of the British in October 1812, the family decided to evacuate, leaving Louis Hasbrouck behind to tend to his law practice. Catherine's sister Sarah Lasher expressed concern for Nanny in her advanced pregnancy being at a battlefront.[16]

A few weeks after the family arrived in Hurley, on November 13, 1812, Nanny delivered a baby boy. Catherine wrote, "[Nanny] Nurses as boldly as you please. I cannot think of taking her back with her white brat and no doubt another as soon as possible. I have not mentioned it yet for I have hardly seen her. I cannot stomach it."[17]

When Nanny became aware of Catherine's plans to get rid of her, she openly argued with Catherine and begged to go back to Ogdensburg to be with the father of her child. Considering that Nanny had cared for Catherine through the births and laying in of three of Catherine's daughters, she may have felt entitled to some sympathy from her mistress. Unfortunately, Catherine wrote, she was outraged that a slave would talk to her so and doubly so when Nanny refused to reveal the name of the father of the baby.

On September 23, 1813, Louis Hasbrouck sold Nanny and her male child to Thomas Jansen of Shawangunk, Ulster County. The sale lists her as his enslaved person but limits the terms of her indenture to ten years. Her ten-month-old son (who was never given a name) was to serve the term of service "as the law regulates"—in other words, until he was twenty-one.

On June 10, 1814, in Ulster County, Louis Hasbrouck purchased a male enslaved person named "Sharp" from Alden (Aldert?) Roosa for $300. (Upon emancipation, Sharp took the name Joseph Sharp.) Joseph was

Thomas Jansen's house, Shawangunk, Ulster County. *Photograph by Bryan Thompson, October 2019.*

Bill of sale for "Sharp," enslaved person of Louis Hasbrouck. *Hasbrouck Family Papers, Ogdensburg Public Library Special Collections.*

probably part of Alden Roosa's inheritance from his father, Andries Roosa. In the will, the elder Roosa freed one enslaved man, "Bill," but divided "the remaining negroes and negro wenches" in his possession among his three children, Mary Shaw, Alden Roosa and Levi Roosa.[18] These enslaved people are listed in Andries's will, but no enslaved people are listed in his possession at the time of the 1800 census.

Joseph Sharp's terms of service were for ten years. Hasbrouck brought Joseph Sharp to live in Ogdensburg. He served as a general servant about the house as Louis Hasbrouck was often absent on business. In June 1817, Louis wrote to Catherine: "I wish you would let Sharp plant some more beans in the quarter acre opposite the asparagus bed....Please tell Sharp to put the wagon out of the weather in the barn. And after helping you as much as you want, let him attend to his clearing on the new lot."[19] Joseph Sharp eventually gained his freedom and is listed in the 1830 Oswegatchie census as head of a household with five free Black people: one male under ten, one male thirty-six to fifty-four, two females under ten and one female fifty-five to ninety-nine.

## ENSLAVED PEOPLE DIFFICULT TO TRACK

Joseph Sharp is just one example of an uncounted enslaved person in St. Lawrence County. There are certainly many more who were missed.

Ownership of a person in the first part of the nineteenth century in New York was a symbol of high social status. For example, William Cooper, landholder and the father of the novelist James Fenimore Cooper, owned a house servant named Joseph Stuart. Stuart often accompanied Cooper on his travels and most certainly accompanied him during his early trips to De Kalb in St. Lawrence County.

By 1810, the U.S. census for St. Lawrence County does show seventeen households with enslaved people in them. (See appendix A.) This is certainly an undercount. Louis Hasbrouck's enslaved people illustrate this, since they are listed in Ulster County, where he was wintering. David and Rebecca Ogden's enslaved people are also listed at their winter residence. Early histories of Ogdensburg describe Nathan Ford, first judge of St. Lawrence County, as owning one person named Black Dick. Dick does not appear on the 1810 St. Lawrence County census. David Ford's enslaved person Jude is not listed either. Smith Stillwell is credited by an *Ogdensburg Journal* article with owning one person, "Black Betty," but she too is not listed in 1810. She may be the individual listed on the 1850 census for De Peyster as Susan Wadsworth, age one hundred.

The situation is not helped by the fact that the actual census pages enumerating free and enslaved Black people in St. Lawrence County in 1820 no longer exist. Only the abstracts of totals by town survive. It is telling that the detailed enumeration of each town for white citizens has survived, but those details for the county's Black citizens were discarded.

The fact that enslaved people are seldom mentioned in records of the time illustrates that they were treated as you would a horse or any other property, mentioned only when it was necessary. Louis Hasbrouck's brother Joseph only casually mentioned his enslaved people once in passing in the many letters to Louis. This was when he suffered a catastrophic loss when one of his servants ran away while he was sick and could not be found in New York or Boston.[20]

Another example is set at a hotel during a trip to De Kalb. Isaac Cooper owned a person referred to only as "your black man" in a letter of March 16, 1813, from a Mr. Gregory of Albany to Cooper.[21] It seems that Cooper's man was suspected of stealing William's hat (William was Mr. Gregory's manservant). This was a gentleman's hat costing six or seven dollars and had been given to William by Lieutenant Fredrick De Peyster. It had been replaced by a shabby, worn-out hat. The exchange was witnessed by another man's servant. A pair of blue broadcloth pantaloons was also missing. Gregory was not sure if Isaac Cooper's man had the articles but wanted

Cooper to check. If he did not see the items, Cooper was instructed to say nothing, as Gregory did not want to wrongly accuse a man.

Another place that unrecorded enslaved people can be identified is in legal documents. For example, Salmon Rich had used his slave as collateral in a $500 loan from his widowed mother, Mary. After the loan was made, Mary remarried a man named Simeon Benjamin, and all her property, including the family slave, became his.

We learn about Salmon Rich's slave in a letter from John Fine to Isaac Cooper in November 1815: "I omitted to mention to you that in the settlement with Benjamin it is wished you would ask for the bill of sale of a negro boy, given by Young Rich to induce Benjamin to exempt Thrall's Mill seat from his mortgage. This is the only personal property Rich has."[22]

The enslaved person, whose name we never learn in the documents, may have gone to live and work for Benjamin, or he may have been rented out to some other person for cash. At that time, an adult male enslaved person sold for $200 to $300, the price of a substantial amount of land on the frontier.

There must have been a strong bond between Salmon Rich and "his negro boy." As the 1815 letter notes, "Rich would be glad to give him [Benjamin] a piece of his 100 Acres to retain his boy."[23] This Black man never appears on the census records for St. Lawrence or Otsego Counties with either family.

## EMANCIPATION

All New York State enslaved people were scheduled to be freed by July 4, 1827. By law, no slaves were to be sold out of state after 1799. A $250 fine was the prescribed penalty for such a sale. The historical record, however, demonstrates that sales did occur. One example is Gouverneur Ogden, the largest slaveholder who was a year-round resident of St. Lawrence County. His wife, Charlotte, noted in her diary on March 22, 1827, "Father [Gouverneur] sold the two Blacks for $200, a pretty good bargain; Had a very melancholy parting."[24] Four months before these individuals should have been emancipated, they were illegally deprived of their freedom. There is no record of any fine being levied for this infraction. This document makes the local legend that the Ogdens were Underground Railroad operatives highly unlikely. Somehow, the slave owners who risked legal punishment to save their substantial investment in slaves are now portrayed in local legend as abolitionist heroes.

Local enslaved people who were emancipated began independent lives in St. Lawrence County or left the area. Joseph Sharp, introduced earlier, had two daughters, Jane and Polly, who were still living in Ogdensburg in 1850. At least one Black woman stayed with her former owner. Antoinette Jones, a servant of the Borland family, was born in New York State about 1806. She was living with the families of Charles and John Borland in De Kalb by 1820. From census records, she appears to have continued to live with the family until at least 1855, long after her emancipation. In the 1850 census, she was listed as illiterate.

## CHRISTOPHER RUSH

One of the most notable formerly enslaved persons who spent time in St. Lawrence County was Christopher Rush (also known as Uncle Kit). Rush was born in North Carolina in 1777. He was owned by Isaac Edwards. When Edwards died, his wife, Mary, and two daughters, Rebecca Cornell and Mary, moved to New York City. In 1797, Rebecca Cornell Edwards married David A. Ogden. Christopher Rush and several other enslaved people were included in Rebecca's marriage dowry.

David, along with his uncle Samuel Ogden and his brothers Gouverneur Ogden and Thomas Ludlow Ogden, invested heavily in land in upstate New York, including in St. Lawrence County. Rush's obituary noted, "Uncle Kit frequently made trips with his master up through Albany to the site of the then future city of Ogdensburgh, which at that time consisted of but one building, erected by the British troops for their protection."[25] (British troops continued to occupy the fortifications at Ogdensburg after the end of the American Revolution until the signing of the Jay Treaty in 1794 clarified the boundary between the United States and

Reverend Christopher Rush. *Schomburg Center for Research in Black Culture, Photographs and Prints Division, The New York Public Library. "Rev. Christopher Rush." New York Public Library Digital Collections.*

The Ogden Cottage, Waddington. Built during the time Christopher Rush was enslaved by the Ogdens. *Photo by Bryan Thompson.*

Canada.) David and Rebecca spent their winters in New York City but soon built the Ogden cottage in Waddington, utilizing enslaved labor. In 1810, they built an impressive stone mansion on Ogden Island.

Christopher Rush joined the African Methodist Episcopal (AME) Zion Church in 1803. Sometime before the War of 1812, the Ogdens freed Rush. He traveled south that year and brought his father north to freedom. He was licensed to preach in the AME Zion Church in 1815. He became a deacon in the church in 1822. Rush was instrumental in establishing the Phoenix Society, a Black literary society. He also helped establish other AME Zion churches in New Jersey and Connecticut. In 1828, Christopher Rush became a bishop in the AME Zion Church.

The AME Zion Church became known as the freedom church due to its strong support of the abolitionist movement and the Underground Railroad. Rush was an active agent for the organization, sending freedom seekers to the North through familiar lands. Rush became friends with Frederick Douglass, and Harriet Tubman and Sojourner Truth both became members of the AME Zion Church that Rush helped to lead.

Rush was described as short of stature, reserved in manner and stern in address, with a commanding style of preaching. It was said you could hear him preaching from a block away.

Bishop Christopher Rush died on July 16, 1873, in his ninety-seventh year. Over three thousand people attended his funeral in New York City, filling the streets for a block surrounding his church. Nearly ten thousand passed by his coffin during the viewing.

## THE LAVINIA BAKER BOSTON AND RICHARD BOSTON FAMILY

The Bostons, a Black family of Massena, were a presence in the area from the time of the early settlement of the town through the 1860s. Legend has it that Richard Boston arrived in Massena with his master, Daniel Robinson, in the winter of 1803–4, settling on or near Robinson's Bay. Both Robinson and Richard Boston were born in Worcester County, Massachusetts, and had lived in Vermont before arriving in Massena.

Lavinia Baker married Richard Boston on December 5, 1809, at the Trinity Anglican Church in Cornwall, Upper Canada. Lavinia Baker was the daughter of Dorine Baker and a Dutch or German soldier, Jacob Baker.

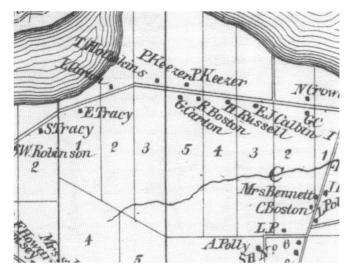

The Robinson Bay area of the town of Massena showing the Robinson farm and the two Boston brothers farms. *From* New Topographical Atlas of St. Lawrence County from Actual Surveys by S.N. and D.G. Beers and Assistants *(1865; reprinted Churchville, NY: B and E Printers, Martin Wehle, 1976).*

Dorine was the enslaved person of the Colonel James Gray family. Hence, all of her children were by law the property of the Gray family even though their father was a free white man.[26]

When the Gray family moved to Gray's Creek near Cornwall, Upper Canada, in 1784, they brought Dorine Baker's family with them. Lavinia was born at Gray's Creek. In 1795, Colonel Gray died, and Dorine and her children became the property of his son Robert Isaac Gray.

Robert Isaac Gray died in a shipwreck on Lake Ontario in 1804. In a will he made in that year, he stated, "I feel it is my duty incumbent on me, in consequence of the long and faithful service of Dorine, my black woman servant, rendered to my family, to release, manumit and discharge her from the state of slavery in which she now is, and to give her and all her children their freedom." The fourth clause of the will added:

> *And in order that provisions may be made for the said Dorine and her children, and that she may not want after my decease, my will is, and I hereby empower my executors, out of my real estate to raise the sum of twelve hundred pounds currency, and place the same in some solvent and secure fund, and the interest arising from the same I give and bequeath to said Dorine, her heirs and assigns forever, to be paid annually.*

The executors of the will elected to instead give the Bakers 2,150 acres of land, which were sold and the proceeds divided between Dorine and her surviving children, including Lavinia.[27]

On May 2, 1820, Richard and Lavinia Boston entered into a mortgage with Daniel Robinson[28] to purchase 22½ acres of land for $135. They had until September 1, 1824, to raise the money. A deed for the land was recorded on June 21, 1820.[29] Contrary to legend, this appears as a purchase agreement, not as a gift from Richard Boston's former master. It is more than likely that this purchase was made possible through the bequest that Lavinia received. The benevolence of Daniel and Esther Robinson may have been in their willingness to sell property to a Black family.

By 1835, Richard Boston was one of only two Black men in St. Lawrence County eligible to vote. The other was his son Jacob. The low number of Black voters was due to an 1826 law granting universal voting rights to all white men. The same act, the year before the 1827 emancipation, raised the amount of property Black men needed to be eligible to vote from $50 to $250. In 1827, New York State law made the Black suffrage barrier even higher by requiring a three-year residency with no debts owed in order to vote.

Richard and Lavinia purchased an additional fifty acres of land in 1842. The Bostons did well enough economically that they are listed as donors of wheat and corn to a local campaign to fight famine in Scotland and Ireland in June 1847. Richard Boston died sometime before March 15, 1858, when his heirs, Jacob Boston, Charles Boston and Lavinia McDonnell, sold their interest in his land to their brother Richard Boston Jr.

Each of the Bostons' sons is listed on the census records in St. Lawrence County as mulatto. They each married white women. Two of Richard and Lavinia Boston's grandsons served in the Civil War in white units, passing as white. J.P. Boston enlisted in the 106th New York Infantry at the age of sixteen in September 1864, and Simon Boston enlisted in the 61st New York Infantry at the age of seventeen in August 1864.

The late eighteenth and early nineteenth centuries were years of slow movement from slavery to freedom under gradual emancipation for many Black pioneers of St. Lawrence County, since slavery did not end until 1827. Many Black residents were hindered in advancement by the reluctance of white residents to sell land to Black people. Nonetheless, some of these pioneers established intergenerational families and emerged as community leaders.

## Timeline, Chapter 2

| | |
|---|---|
| 1797 | Nathan Ford settles in Old Fort Oswegatchie with the enslaved man Dick. |
| 1799 | New York State passes the "Act for the Gradual Abolition of Slavery." |
| 1800 | David Ford visits Fort Oswegatchie accompanied by Christopher Rush. |
| 1801 | Thomas Jefferson becomes third president of the United States. |
| 1802 | St. Lawrence County is incorporated. |
| 1802 | Louis Hasbrouck comes to county as first county clerk. |
| 1803 | Richard Boston arrives in Massena. |
| 1804 | Louis Hasbrouck brings his family to live in Ogdensburg, accompanied by an enslaved woman, Nanny. |
| 1804 | Dorine Baker and her children are freed. |
| 1805 December | David Ford swears oath to bring enslaved child Jude to St. Lawrence County. |
| 1807 December | Embargo Act goes into effect. |
| 1809 | James Madison becomes president. |
| 1809 December 5 | Lavinia Baker marries Richard Boston at Cornwall. |
| 1812 June | Local militia called up in Ogdensburg. |

| | |
|---|---|
| 1812 June | War is declared with Britain. |
| 1812 October 4 | British attack on Ogdensburg repulsed. |
| 1812 October | Catherine Hasbrouck with her four children and Nanny leave for Ulster County. |
| 1812 November 13 | Nanny gives birth to a male child. |
| 1813 February 22 | British capture Ogdensburg. |
| 1813 September 23 | Louis Hasbrouck sells Nanny and her male child. |
| 1814 June 10 | Louis Hasbrouck buys the enslaved man Sharp. |
| 1815 February 17 | War of 1812 ends. |
| 1815 | Christopher Rush licensed to preach. |
| 1817 | Gradual emancipation extended to those born before 1799. |
| 1817 | James Monroe becomes president. |
| 1817 | Construction of the Erie Canal begins. |
| 1820 May 2 | Lavinia and Richard Boston enter purchase agreement for farm in Massena. |
| 1824 | Sharp's enslavement ends. As a free man, he is known as Joseph Sharp. |
| 1825 | John Q. Adams becomes president. |

| | |
|---|---|
| 1825 | Erie Canal completed. |
| 1826 | Black suffrage in New York State restricted by law requiring $250 property to vote. |
| 1827 | Additional Black voting restrictions requiring three-year residency passed. |
| 1827 March 22 | Gouverneur Ogden illegally sells his last two slaves. |
| 1827 July 4 | All enslaved adult Black people in state freed. Those under twenty-one serve indenture until they are twenty-one. |
| 1828 | Christopher Rush becomes a bishop in the AME Zion Church. |

CHAPTER 3

# THE ABOLITIONIST ERA (1827–1865)

## BLACK ABOLITIONIST PREACHERS, LANDOWNERS AND CIVIL WAR VOLUNTEERS

S lavery officially ended in New York State on July 4, 1827. However, the gradual abolition process had a devastating impact on Black citizens throughout the state. Illegal sales of slaves before they would have been legally free led to decline in the Black population in the state. The prolonged emancipation process also had serious economic impacts on the Black community that remained. The $250 property and three-year residency requirement restricted Black suffrage for the next generation to the Boston family, introduced in the previous chapter.

In 1846, when a constitutional amendment to end this restriction on Black male suffrage was put to the voters, St. Lawrence County voted down the measure: 4,867 opposed ending the restrictions, while 2,585 supported ending them.

Despite these setbacks, this era was a time of rising expectations for the Black community in the state. Although state law said only that school commissioners "may" form schools for "colored" children, some local schools allowed Black children to attend the local common schools. At least one local Black scholar graduated from the St. Lawrence Academy in Potsdam, and several Black ministers preached throughout the county. The local abolitionist movement was active by 1834 and grew from a small minority to an overwhelming majority of the white community by the 1850s.

In this chapter, we will look at the lives of some of the local Black citizens who were leaders in the abolitionist movement as well as a local family whose future was profoundly changed by that movement.

# THE BOWLES FAMILY:
## ABOLITIONIST PREACHERS AND FARMERS

In April 1834, Elisha Risdon noted in his diary, "Been to Society meeting, arranging to hire the Rev. Mr. Bowles." The Congregational Church of the Town of Hopkinton had agreed to hire Charles Bowles II to preach at its church.

The Congregational Church at Hopkinton. *Photograph by Bryan Thompson.*

The Reverend Charles Bowles II was a Black man who was born in Grafton, New Hampshire, on January 24, 1789. He moved with his father, Reverend Charles Bowles I, a Baptist minister, to Vermont and then to Ashburnham, Massachusetts. He served in the War of 1812. He married Keziah Marsh (1783–1860) in Boston on September 1, 1814. Before coming to Hopkinton, he was a minister in Floyd (Oneida County) and in Bridgewater, New Hampshire.

He arrived with his family in Hopkinton on May 24, 1834. For many of his congregants, he was the first Black professional they had ever encountered. Within a year, Reverend Bowles dedicated a new Congregational meetinghouse in Hopkinton.

Reverend Bowles preached well beyond Hopkinton. Within a few months, he was also speaking in the town of Lawrence. From 1836 to 1838, his ministry included the Presbyterian (Congregational) Church in Depo sic (later Lisbon). While he was living in Hopkinton, his son Charles Bowles III attended the St. Lawrence Academy (now State University of New York at Potsdam), graduating in 1837.[30]

Early in Reverend Charles Bowles II's ministry in Hopkinton, Elisha Risdon noted in his diary on September 14, 1834, "Mr. Bowles preached on infant baptism today." This was probably the same sermon that the Reverend Bowles published in 1841 right after he left Hopkinton to preach at the Congregational Church of Pharsalia (Chenango County). "A Sermon on the Covenant of Grace Which God Made with Abraham" is his only surviving intellectual work. In the introduction, he states, "I was brought up a Baptist and know by unhappy experience all the difficulties which are thrown in front of the young convert." The work shows an almost adolescent rebellion against his father's Baptist beliefs.

In 1842, Charles Bowles II became the first minister of the new Congregational Church in West Potsdam (town of Potsdam). By 1843, he was in New South Berlin (Chenango County). From late 1843 to 1846, he served the Stowes Square Presbyterian Church in Lowville (Lewis County). From 1846 to 1849, he served the Lowville Presbyterian Church. He then moved for one year to the Ellisburg Presbyterian Church (Jefferson County). His last assignment was the East Pitcairn Presbyterian Church (town of Pitcairn). He died there on July 29, 1850, at the age of sixty-one.

Perhaps the most important thing the Reverend Bowles II did while he was in Hopkinton was to bring his father to St. Lawrence County. On December 13, 1835, Elisha Risdon noted in his diary, "Mr. Bowles father preaches today. All but myself at meeting." Was Elisha sick, or did he object to a Baptist preacher in his Congregational church?

The Reverend Charles Bowles I was a seventy-five-year-old Black Freewill Baptist minister who had spent much of his career preaching in northwestern Vermont. He was born in either Boston or Hanover, Massachusetts, in 1761, the son of an African and the daughter of Colonel Morgan. Bowles I joined the Continental army in 1775. He served five terms in the Massachusetts and New Hampshire lines. He was discharged as a private in Newburgh in November 1782.

Shortly after his American Revolution service, Charles Bowles married Mary Corliss. The young couple made their home in Warner, New Hampshire, where ten children were born to them. Against his Congregational wife's wishes, Bowles joined the local Calvinist Baptist church.

In 1780, in New Durham, New Hampshire, George Whitefield organized the first Northern Freewill Baptist Church. The Freewill Baptists rejected the Calvinist notion of predestination. Instead, their adherents believed each member must make his own place in heaven through living a good life and doing good works while on earth.

Within ten years of the group's organization, they banned slave owners from membership. In 1827, they banned segregation in their ministry and their congregations. In 1835, they passed four resolutions against slavery, including one that required their members to "frequently and fervently pray for the abolition of Slavery" by making such a prayer part of their weekly liturgy. Another required them as "Christians…to use their best exertions in their respective states to procure the abolition of slavery." In 1850, following the passage of the Fugitive Slave Act, they passed another resolution: "We will do all we can, consistent with…the bible, to prevent the recapture of the fugitive, and to aid him in his efforts to escape."[31] Many from the church became political agitators for the end of slavery. Members of the group, such as George McEwen of the town of Lawrence, bragged about their activities with the Underground Railroad.[32]

Charles Bowles I soon left the Calvinist Baptist Church to join the newly organized Northern Freewill Baptist Church. He was called to the ministry but resisted, going to sea for three years.

In 1813, he began working as a lay preacher in Glocester, Rhode Island, where he was the subject of mob violence for preaching to white audiences. In an early act of passive resistance, when the mob entered his meeting, he and all his congregants held hands in a circle of prayer. The mob did not know how to react and soon dispersed.

In 1816, he moved with his family to Huntington, Vermont. He was officially ordained there on November 26, 1816. It was not easy being a Black preacher in rural Vermont at that time. At one of his early meetings in Hinesburg, Vermont, a crowd of face-painted revelers came to break up his meeting. They came prepared with a rail to drown him. His reaction was to calmly announce:

> *I am informed that there are certain persons in this house, who have agreed to put me on a wooden horse, carry me to the pond and throw me in; and now dear creatures, I shall make no resistance at all—I am already; but before starting I have one request to make. I wish you to put one of your most resolute men forward, because I have another subject from God to preach on the way; and we will have music as we go along, glory be to God, yes we will have music; glory be to God.*[33]

He soon converted many of the mob, and they were baptized in Lake Champlain.

One of his early Vermont converts was a young woman named Clarissa Danforth. She felt the urge to join the ministry and began preaching to male audiences in December 1816. This was even more outrageous than a Black man ministering to them. She was roundly ridiculed by a Dr. Clark, who said, "If an Ass could reprove the prophet Balaam, and a barn-yard fowl could reprove Peter, may not a woman rebuke sin?"[34] In a generous act of support against a type of prejudice he knew too well, the Reverend Charles Bowles I joined the Reverend Clarissa Danforth in preaching a joint sermon on January 23, 1817. For many years thereafter, the pair often appeared together at services.

Despite opposition, Reverend Bowles continued his ministry and won many converts by his unconventional methods. He would go door to door knocking and asking each family to spend a few minutes in prayer with him. With his genial character and strong intellect, he soon disarmed most racial opposition.

By the time Charles Bowles II began his ministry in Hopkinton, his father had already been circuit riding in Clinton County. Two days before Charles Bowles II moved his family into their Hopkinton home, Charles Bowles I gave up his home in Huntington, Vermont, and began a year of itinerate preaching in Rutland, Vermont. He gradually moved his door-to-door revival closer to his son's town, bringing his young widowed daughter Elinor Preston and her two children with him. He preached his way across northern Vermont and New York. On December 13, 1835, he preached at his son's Congregational church in Hopkinton.

On January 10, 1836, Reverend Charles Bowles I purchased the Tyler Gove farm[35] southeast of the village of Hopkinton, supposedly in order to retire. His vision was failing. He set up his daughter and grandchildren to support themselves on the farm. But he soon began his door-to-door ministry as his old friends from Vermont living in the area called on him. Within a year, he had established a Freewill Baptist group near Dickinson, in a section called Burnt Hill, in the town of Lawrence. A second group soon began meeting in a barn in Lawrence. He preached wherever he could, led from meeting to meeting on his horse by willing parishioners. He was remembered as a powerful speaker, six feet tall, with a deep heavy voice, citing the Bible, chapter and verse, from memory as his eyes failed.

A description of a visit to the Howard schoolhouse in the town of Pierrepont provides an interesting anecdote of his amazing powers of recognition.

> *Elder William Whitfield a licensed minister, then living in Lawrence, (a brother that Elder Bowles had never seen, but only heard his voice) came into the Howard school-house while Elder Bowles was preaching; after sermon, several brethren and sisters spoke in exhortation. Elder Whitfield, as an entire stranger in the meeting, rose up and began to speak; as soon as he had done speaking, Elder Bowles exclaimed, brother Whitfield, will you come forward and close the meeting. He knew brother Whitfield readily by his voice, though he did not know until then that he was in the town.*[36]

At the same place, a Brother Crary of the Wesleyan faith, "alluding to the American prejudice against color; turning to Elder Bowles in the presence of the audience, he remarked, that no doubt Elder Bowles regretted that he was a colored man. Elder Bowles' countenance lit up with pleasure, as he answered with a strong and emphatic, 'No! Never. Hundreds have been led to Christ and converted just by my color.'"[37]

The Reverend Charles Bowles I sold his farm on April 11, 1839, and moved to Dickinson in the town of Lawrence to return to full-time ministry. He was seventy-eight years old. By then, he had seen the Freewill Baptist denomination grow to include two congregations in Lawrence and congregations in Pierrepont, Stockholm, West Parishville and Nicholville.

In August 1837, local members of his Freewill Baptist churches were instrumental in calling for and establishing the St. Lawrence County Antislavery Society. By 1840, there were Freewill Baptist churches in Brasher, Lawrence, Parishville, Hopkinton, Stockholm, West Potsdam, Pierrepont, Morley, Hermon, De Kalb, South Hammond and West Fowler. In that year, the Lawrence quarterly meeting, held at Nicholville, passed a resolution condemning slavery. The Reverend Charles Bowles I's gentle, commanding, intellectual presence left none whom he touched in doubt of the humanity of his race.

The Reverend Charles W. Bowles I died on March 16, 1843, and was laid to rest in the Constableville cemetery under an impressive headstone paid for by his admiring parishioners. In a fitting testament to his memory, in the November 1844 presidential election, the citizens of Lawrence cast eighty-two votes for James Birney, candidate of the Liberty Party, an early abolitionist party. The Freewill Baptists of St. Lawrence County, which he had established, continued to agitate for the end to slavery and to aid fugitives until the end of the Civil War.

A grandson, Charles H. Bowles III, was born in Massachusetts in 1816. As mentioned before, he graduated from the St. Lawrence Academy, probably one of the school's first Black graduates. After graduation, he taught for two years at the Abrams District School in Hopkinton. He was noted as a strict disciplinarian.

In January 1846, his father, Charles Bowles II, bought a thirty-four-acre farm in Pitcairn.[38] Charles Bowles III took up residence there and began to build a farm in the wilderness. His parents joined him in 1850, but his father soon died. His mother, Keziah, moved to Iowa, where she died in 1860.

In 1852, Charles Bowles III married Clarissa Blank. They had one child, a daughter named Mariah. Mariah died sometime after her eighth birthday. Clarissa died in 1885.

In 1888, Charles Bowles III had no surviving family members and was suffering from dementia. A local jury declared him mentally incompetent

Tombstone of the Reverend Charles Bowles I in Constableville. *Photograph by Bryan Thompson.*

and had his property seized. A notice in the April 6, 1888 *St. Lawrence Herald* commented, "Mr. Bowles was a college-bred man, and the correctness of his language contrasts queerly with the wandering ideas it conveys." Charles Bowles III died at the St. Lawrence Psychiatric Hospital on June 21, 1897. He is buried in the East Pitcairn cemetery.

With their lives, three generations of the Bowles family demonstrated the intellectual equality and humanity of their race to their neighbors in St. Lawrence County.

## The Fry Family of Gouverneur:
## Black Pioneers of St. Lawrence County

The blatant inequality of New York State removing the property ownership requirement of $50 for all white male voters in 1822, while increasing the property ownership requirement for Black male voters to $250, was an ongoing irritation for New York's abolitionists. In 1846, they managed to get a constitutional amendment on the ballot to remove this barrier to Black suffrage. The proposed amendment was resoundingly defeated.

Gerrit Smith, the noted abolitionist and philanthropist land baron, decided to take measures into his own hands. He announced that he would give fifty-acre parcels of land to two free Black men in every county in the state so they could vote. He instructed his agents to select the candidates throughout the state.

The two people who were selected in St. Lawrence County were John King and Flora Fry of Gouverneur. One of these was, in fact, a woman. Flora Fry was granted the southwest quarter of lot number 336, in Township 11, of Essex County. Although no official deed is recorded in Essex County to Flora Fry from Gerrit Smith, many of the Timbuktu grantees signed over their title claims in lieu of getting a deed. This sale of claim allowed the almost penniless Flora Fry to become a homeowner in Gouverneur.

Who was Flora Fry, and why was she given a Gerrit Smith land grant when women of any race would not be able to vote in New York State until 1918?

Flora Fry was born Flora Buck around 1800 in New York State, probably in the town of Champion (Jefferson County), the daughter of Benjamin Buck. Benjamin Buck settled in Champion in 1795. He worked for Jean Baptiste Bossout operating a ferry across the Black River at Long Falls (later Carthage).

By 1823, Flora Buck had married Danby Fry; their first child, Ursula, was born in that year.[39] In 1830, at the time of the U.S. census, Danby and Flora Fry were living with their family in the town of Philadelphia (Jefferson County). The family had grown to include three girls and one boy, all under the age of ten.

In 1835, Danby and Flora Fry were living in the town of LeRay (Jefferson County) with three females and one male, all under the age of sixteen. They owned one neat cow and two hogs.[40]

Sometime after the 1835 New York State census, the Fry family moved back to the town of Philadelphia, where their last child, Danby Fry Jr., was born[41] about 1839. Sometime before 1840, Danby Fry Sr. died and Flora Fry moved to Gouverneur, where she appears on the 1840 census as a head of household with two males under ten, one female under ten and one female in the ten to twenty-four age category. (Her oldest daughter, Ursula, does not appear to have made the move to St. Lawrence County.) Flora, who was sometimes listed as a washerwoman or a farmer, was living in her own household between the households of Harmon VanBuren and Joel Keyes.

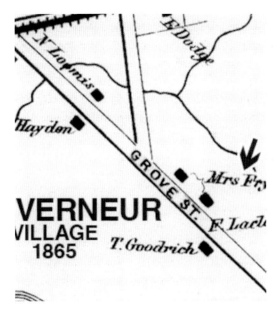

Map of the village of Gouverneur showing Flora Fry's home. *From* New Topographical Atlas of St. Lawrence County from Actual Surveys by S.N. and D.G. Beers and Assistants *(1865; reprinted Churchville, NY: B and E Printers, Martin Wehle, 1976).*

Flora and her descendants continued to live in the Gouverneur area for sixty-five years. Neither she nor any of her five children ever attended school, and none of them could read or write. This was not uncommon for low-income families of this era. Although schools were publicly supported, students still had to provide their own books and other in-kind materials, such as firewood, in order to attend. This was often beyond the means of poor families. Local schools could provide schooling for Black children but were not required to do so. The records they left are scarce, but we can catch a glimpse in census records.

By 1850, Flora Fry was living with her two youngest children, Danby, age ten, and Charlotte, fifteen, on Grove Street in the village of Gouverneur. This was probably the 143 Grove Street home that Flora received a deed for on February 10, 1854. At that time, the house was on the edge of the village with no other dwellings within a block or two. Being on the edge of the village, the family kept two cows and in 1860 produced one hundred pounds of butter.

In 1850, as with many poor families of the time, Flora's two older children were living and working in other households in Gouverneur. Twenty-four-year-old Margery was living in the household of Richard Parsons, a Main Street tinsmith.[42] Fifteen-year-old Robert Fry was living on John Street in the household of Sylvanius Cone, clothier. Robert was a laborer in Cone's fulling mill.

In 1850, Flora's oldest daughter, Ursula, had just married Thomas Johnson and was living in the city of Auburn, New York. Ursula continued to live in Auburn for the next fifty years and raised a family there. In 1855, Ursula's sister Charlotte Fry was living with her in Auburn. By 1860, Charlotte married Bosgert C.P. Freeman. She died soon after.

Robert Fry left Gouverneur by June 1863, when he registered for the draft in Victor (Ontario County). He was employed as a hostler or groom at the time. By 1870, he was living in New York City and was employed as a hostler. Robert spent the rest of his life in the city working as a groom. He never married and died there in May 1909.

By 1860, the only members of the Fry family still in Gouverneur were Margery Fry, laundress, and her brother Danby. There are no records of Flora Fry after her 1854 purchase of the house on Grove Street. She had certainly died by 1866, when Ursula Fry Johnson granted a quitclaim deed to the Grove Street house to her sister Margery.

Danby Fry continued to live in Gouverneur with Margery until November 1863. Meanwhile, in that year important changes in the role of Northern Black men in the Civil War were unfolding. Soon Danby found himself in the middle of the changes.

With the Emancipation Proclamation, in January 1863, for the first time Northern Black men were welcomed into the army and subject to the draft. In the spring of 1863, the governors of Massachusetts, Connecticut and Pennsylvania approved the formation of new "colored" regiments from their states.[43] New York's newly elected Governor Horatio Seymour was a staunch opponent of the abolition of slavery and opposed allowing Black men to bear arms or collect military bounties. Seymour would not authorize the organization of a colored regiment from New York State.

On May 3, 1863, various New York dignitaries, including, among others, Horace Greeley, met in New York City and organized the Association for Promoting Colored Volunteering. They petitioned President Abraham Lincoln on June 9, 1863, to allow formation of a New York State colored regiment. Lincoln and Secretary of War Edwin Stanton refused until the organization could show in writing that Governor Seymour would not form a regiment. The group petitioned Governor Seymour on July 9.

On July 13, the infamous draft riots in New York City broke out. For three days, the city was in chaos. Ironically, the rioters, resentful of the new draft, turned their anger on the Black citizens of the city as cause for their woes. Hundreds of the very men who Governor Seymour was keeping from enlisting or being drafted were killed or injured by the angry mob.

New York State abolitionists, known as the Fremont League, met in Poughkeepsie on July 15 and 16. In reaction to the recent draft riots in New York City, they decided to show that New York's Black population was ready and willing to stand in defense of its country. In early August 1863, they sent out recruiters to all the counties in the state to sign up Black volunteers. One of the volunteers these recruiters signed up was Danby Fry of Gouverneur.

Meanwhile, the Association for Promoting Colored Volunteering, not having heard back from Governor Seymour, authorized Lewis Francis to petition him again on August 13, 1863. By early October, Seymour had still not replied in any manner to any of the petitions to raise a colored regiment. The association next authorized a Mr. Requ of Albany to personally call on Seymour with the petition. At last, Seymour put his intention not to form a colored regiment into writing. The governor claimed the federal government was in no need of additional regiments. With this information in hand, the association was able to petition the secretary of war for authorization to raise a colored regiment from New York State.

After a very successful public meeting on November 16, 1863, free drilling rooms were set up on Broadway in New York City. The August volunteers were encouraged to congregate in the city in anticipation of the formation of the first New York colored regiment.

Secretary of War Stanton approved the formation of a regiment on November 21, 1863, but "required the application of suitable persons." The Association for Promoting Colored Volunteering was not an acceptable organization, so they joined the Union League, an already established organization for the support of New York troops. The Union League was finally authorized to raise a company of colored volunteers on December 3, 1863. After further haggling, N.B. Bartrum, a former New York City public school vice principal, was appointed brigadier general of the Twentieth United States Colored Troops (USCT).

While all this was going on, Danby Fry was making his way to New York City. The five-foot-five-and-a-half-inch-tall, hazel-eyed Danby presented himself at the Broadway office of the Union League on December 1, 1863. He was enlisted by Captain Duffy. Danby was so enthusiastic that he signed up two days before the organization of the Twentieth was officially sanctioned.

These early enlistees did not have an easy time. Most of them were swindled out of their enlistment bounties by their enlistment officers. Eventually, three of these officers went to jail for their crimes, but no financial restitution was ever made to the recruits.

```
       20    U.S.C.T.

Danby Fry

........., Co. ..6, 20 Reg't U.S. Col'd Inf.
Appears on
       Company Descriptive Book
of the organization named above.
       DESCRIPTION.
Age 2/ years; height 5 feet 5/4 inches.
Complexion    Colored
Eyes  Hazel ; hair  Black
Where born    N.Y.
Occupation    Boatman
       ENLISTMENT.
When    Dec 1st        , 186 3
Where    N.Y. City
By whom Capt Duffy ; term 3 y'rs.
Remarks: Corpl Mch-12-65
```

Service record of Danby Fry. *Fry,
Lavinia, Widow's Pension File # 362810.
The Civil War Widows' Pension Files.
The U.S. National Archives and Records
Administration, Washington, D.C.*

The new enlistees of the Twentieth Infantry USCT were mustered for duty on February 9, 1864, at Rikers Island. To get to the island, they were forced to pay a bribe to the ferrymen the army had hired to transport them. Danby and his cohorts were reported by the local press to be training enthusiastically for their new responsibilities.

The Twentieth Infantry USCT completed its basic training on March 5, 1864. Danby Fry and his fellow troops were transported to 26th Street in New York City. In a demonstration of the change in attitudes since the July race riots, they were given a grand sendoff by many of the most notable dignitaries of the city. Accompanied by an army band—a substitute band, as the regular New York City army band refused to play for colored troops—the men of the Twentieth marched to Union Square, where they were applauded in speech after speech and given hampers of gifts by a committee of city women that included Mrs. John Jacob Astor.

That afternoon, Danby Fry and his regiment left for New Orleans in the Gulf of Mexico war zone. From New Orleans, they were sent to Port Hudson, Louisiana. In April, they were sent to Point Cavallo, Texas. By July 1864, they were stationed in Plaquemine, Louisiana. The Twentieth soon moved to Camp Parapet, a former Confederate base one mile north of New Orleans, where they stayed until December 1864. The regiment was then sent to Pascagoula, Florida, until February 1865. They next moved to Nashville, Tennessee. On March 12, 1865, Danby Fry was promoted to corporal.

In June, the regiment was sent back to New Orleans. While in New Orleans, Danby Fry developed a respiratory condition. He was hospitalized

Widow's pension application of Lavinia Fry. *Fry, Lavinia, Widow's Pension File # 362810. The Civil War Widows' Pension Files. The U.S. National Archives and Records Administration, Washington, D.C.*

on August 31 and remained in the hospital until October 5. Danby was mustered out with his company at New Orleans on October 7, 1865. He was treated at the army hospital one more time on October 11, 1865, before returning home to New York State.[44]

When Danby Fry returned home, he found his way to Auburn, New York, where in March 1866 he married Lavinia Gatewood. Danby worked as a coachman and servant in the community, but he continued to suffer from the respiratory ailment he had contracted during his service in the Civil War. He died in Auburn on February 2, 1883, and is buried in the North Street Cemetery. Lavinia Fry was denied a widow's pension in 1888 because army medical records did not state a cause for Danby's hospitalization.

While her siblings struck out into the larger world, Margery Fry remained at her mother's Grove Street home. She must have been doing relatively well for herself; in 1867 and 1869, she purchased additional adjoining land from Edwin Dodge to expand her village lot to almost one acre. She continued to keep a cow, sell butter and do laundry to make a living.

While Margery remained in her Grove Street home, racial attitudes in the area were changing and hardening in the late nineteenth century. Not once in her lifetime did her name appear in the local newspapers, although she lived and worked in the community for over sixty years. She never married and was always listed as living alone from the time her brother left for war.

According to Margery's own responses on the 1900 census, she was born in June 1824. In late 1903, at almost eighty years old and after a lifetime of hard labor, her health was failing. She moved to the city of Troy (Rensselaer County) to live with her niece Emma Berry. Margery died there on February 17, 1905.[45]

We will probably never know why Gerrit Smith granted the land in Essex County to Flora Fry. However, the results of that grant are clearly evident. For two generations, the previously indigent Fry family were property owners and self-supporting residents of the Gouverneur community.

The Grove Street address where the Fry family lived in Gouverneur. *Photograph by Bryan Thompson.*

Despite legal barriers as the century proceeded, the citizens of St. Lawrence County brushed shoulders with or read about African American neighbors who preached sermons in local churches, owned property and ran small businesses. Local African Americans were joined by some white neighbors in advocating for the abolition of slavery and then served in the war to end it.

## TIMELINE, CHAPTER 3

| | |
|---|---|
| 1775 | Charles Bowles I joins Massachusetts militia. |
| 1782 | Charles Bowles I is discharged from Continental army after serving five terms. |
| 1800 | Flora Buck born. |
| 1816 | Charles Bowles I ordained as Freewill Baptist minister. |
| 1824 June | Margery Fry born in Jefferson County, New York. |
| 1827 | Slavery in New York State ends. |
| 1827 | Northern Freewill Baptists ban segregation in their ministry and congregations. |
| 1829 | Andrew Jackson sworn in as president of the United States. |
| 1833 | Slavery abolished in most of the British Empire, including Canada. |
| 1834 April | The Congregational church of Hopkinton hires Black minister Charles Bowles II. |
| 1835 December | Charles Bowles I preaches at the Hopkinton Congregational church. |

| | |
|---|---|
| 1836 January | Charles Bowles I buys farm in Hopkinton. |
| 1837 | Martin Van Buren becomes president. |
| 1837 | Charles Bowles III graduates from the St. Lawrence Academy. |
| 1837 August | St. Lawrence County Antislavery Society organized at Potsdam. |
| 1839 April | Charles Bowles I moves to Dickinson to lead a Freewill Baptist congregation. |
| 1839 | Danby Fry Jr. born in Philadelphia, New York. |
| 1840 | Charles Bowles I's circuit riding establishes Freewill Baptist churches throughout the county. |
| 1840 | Flora Fry and her family move to Gouverneur. |
| 1841 April | John Tyler becomes president. |
| 1843 March | Charles Bowles I dies. |
| 1844 November | Freewill Baptists of Lawrence cast eighty-two votes for Birney, Liberty Party presidential candidate. |
| 1845 | James Polk sworn in as president. |
| 1846 | Gerrit Smith announces he will give land to two free Black men from every county so they can vote. |
| 1846 | Flora Fry and John King selected to receive Smith land from St. Lawrence County. |
| 1848 November | Preston King elected to Congress as Buffalo Platform Democrat. |

| | |
|---|---|
| 1849 | Zachary Taylor sworn in as president. |
| 1850 July | Charles Bowles II dies in Pitcairn. |
| 1850 July | Millard Fillmore assumes presidency. |
| 1850 September | Congress passes Fugitive Slave Act. |
| 1853 | Franklin Pierce sworn in as president. |
| 1854 | Flora Fry receives deed to 143 Grove Street house in Gouverneur. |
| 1854 | Kansas Nebraska Act passed. |
| 1857 | James Buchanan sworn in as president. |
| 1861 | Abraham Lincoln sworn in as president. |
| 1861 April | Battle of Fort Sumter, first battle of the Civil War. |
| 1863 December 1 | Danby Fry enlists in Twentieth Infantry USCT. |
| 1865 October 7 | Danby Fry mustered out of army at New Orleans. |
| 1870 | Ratification of the Fifteenth Amendment finally allows New York State Black men to vote without property. |
| 1883 February 2 | Danby Fry dies of lung disease. Buried in unmarked grave in Auburn, New York. |
| 1888 | Danby Fry's widow Lavinia denied widow's pension. |

| | |
|---|---|
| 1897 June | Charles Bowles III dies at St. Lawrence psychiatric hospital. |
| 1903 | Margery Fry leaves Gouverneur to live with a niece in Troy, New York. |
| 1905 February | Margery Fry dies at Troy, New York. |

## CHAPTER 4

# A SHIFTING LANDSCAPE IN THE POSTWAR YEARS (1860–1900)

## CAMP FOLLOWERS, ENTREPRENEURS AND LABORERS

The North's triumph in the Civil War and the constitutional amendments abolishing slavery and granting citizenship and political rights to the freed people seemed to auger a bright future for the nation's Black population. Those changes undoubtedly would have heartened Corporal Danby Fry and Freewill Baptist antislavery advocates. But Margery Fry's invisibility in Gouverneur in the late nineteenth century suggests that racial exclusion continued. In fact, a deepening racism took hold in St. Lawrence County. Ideas and structures commonly associated with the Jim Crow South hemmed in and endangered the lives of African Americans in the county.

While northern New York remained largely agrarian, there were many changes to the Black population of St. Lawrence County following the Civil War. Before the war, Black residents were native-born to New York, New England, Canada and other Middle Atlantic states. Following the war, there was a migration of formerly enslaved individuals from the southern states into the area. One group of immigrants was former Union camp followers.

## THEY BROUGHT BACK SLAVES: CHARLES CLARK AND OTHER CAMP FOLLOWERS

On Sunday, July 2, 1865, a train pulled into Ogdensburg. On board were several freedmen, including Charles Clark and Thomas Boyer. They were accompanying a number of returning Union veterans of the 106th New York Infantry.[46] Charles Clark was accompanying Gilbert Merrithew, while Rollin George Burnham was with Thomas Boyer.

I became interested in these men and Charles Clark, in particular, when I was examining the 1892 New York State census for De Kalb. There, on page eight, was the household of William Hurlbut that included a hired farmhand: Charles Clark, a Black man. William Hurlbut was my grandmother's uncle. More important, my grandparents had purchased Hurlbut's farm in 1906. My father was born in the farmhouse, and I had grown up living three hundred feet from the house, yet I had never heard of Charles Clark.

My curiosity was piqued. Throughout the 1990s, I asked anyone I met who might have known Clark what they knew. Soon a story began to emerge as I did interviews and delved into old records. The story is not always pretty, but it is a real North Country story.

Charles Clark was born in Albemarle County in the Shenandoah Valley of Virginia sometime between 1845 and 1847.

President Abraham Lincoln's Emancipation Proclamation of January 1, 1863, ordered the Union army to "recognize and maintain the freedom of" former slaves. Henceforth, all slaves in areas captured by the advancing Union army would be freed. As the Union army advanced through the South, the proclamation was read to the Black population at each plantation. The 106th New York Infantry soldiers were part of that advance in the Upper South.

In March and April 1864, the 106th was transferred to the 6th Corps of the Union army and soon found themselves under the command of General Philip Sheridan. They left Maryland to join a campaign in the Shenandoah Valley in August 1864.

Because the Shenandoah Valley had been used repeatedly to attack the North, Union leadership decided to render the valley uninhabitable and unable to support an army. This was the first scorched-earth campaign of the war. Every barn, factory, house and mill was destroyed, and all crops were confiscated or destroyed. All freedmen were carried with the Union army as they moved to Petersburg, Virginia, to continue the war effort. The Shenandoah Valley was rendered useless to the Confederate army.

Freedmen like Charles Clark had endured a lifetime of bondage, often without much knowledge of the outside world. Many readily followed their liberators for safety, sustenance and to join the war of liberation. In Clark's case, it may have been more a matter of life and death: stay and starve, or follow the army and live. Camp followers, such as Clark, did odd jobs for the soldiers for food, shelter and compensation.

When the army was quickly disbanded at the close of the war, the freedmen had to readjust and find new homes and occupations. Many accompanied their army friends and liberators home to the North. Gilbert Merrithew, a soldier from De Kalb, befriended Charles Clark. It was with Merrithew that Clark debarked from Ogdensburg for De Kalb that day. Thomas Boyer also came to St. Lawrence County with the returning troops.

It must have been quite a shock for the two southern teenagers to adjust to the cold North Country winters. Both young men went to work immediately as laborers.

Thomas Boyer worked for Rollin Burnham until Burnham left De Kalb in 1870 to homestead in Storm Lake, Iowa. Boyer then went to live with Burnham's cousin John Burnham at Burnham's Hotel in Old De Kalb[47] and worked as a laborer. Boyer disappears from all public records after the 1870 census, and the rest of his story is unknown.

Charlie, as his neighbors knew him, experienced a lifetime working as a hired farmhand in the northwest section of the town of De Kalb. He never strayed far, living on various farms on Maple Ridge Road, River Road and Rock Island Road for sixty years. At first, he worked for Union veteran farmers and their families: Jesse Streeter and Gilbert Merrithew, as well as Merrithew's daughter and son-in-law, Libby and Evan Thomas. It is with the Thomas family that Charlie proudly posed for a photograph on the family porch.

Charles Clark stands proudly among the members of the Evan Thomas family on River Road in the town of De Kalb. *De Kalb Town Historian's Collection, De Kalb Junction, New York.*

Charlie eventually had to find employment outside the circle of his old Union veteran friends. This is the time in his life I know best because of the memories of my informants. And it was in these years when his lot in life seemed to deteriorate. He never married and had no family of his own to care for him. His wages were meager; by the 1920s, he was earning just twenty-five cents for a week's work on a farm.

He spent the last few years of his life working for Roscoe and Grafton Conklin. While he worked for them, he slept in the manger of their dairy barn, and his food was brought to him on a plate to eat in the barn, as he was not considered clean enough to enter a house.

While boys were allowed to meet and speak with Charlie in the barn when with their fathers, girls did not even know he existed,[48] suggesting he did not leave his home in the barn very often. In the sixty years that Charles Clark lived in the town, his name does not appear once in the local news columns.

By the end of 1923, Charles Clark was almost eighty and no longer able to work. He cried when Roscoe Conklin stopped paying him his twenty-five-cent-a-week wages and called the De Kalb overseer of the poor to take him away. The overseer had him committed to the St. Lawrence County Poorhouse in Canton in early January 1924. Charles Clark died of stomach cancer there on March 28, 1926.[49] There is no mention of his

The St. Lawrence County Poorhouse or County Home. *St. Lawrence County Historical Association Archives, Canton, New York.*

passing in the press. He was buried in the Wayside Cemetery in Richville, New York, in the Gilbert Merrithew family plot. His grave was marked with a simple footstone that said only "Charlie." Sometime in the last fifty years, the stone was removed. Today, the freedman Charles Clark lies in an unmarked grave.

## THE TOMPKINS FAMILY OF CANTON

One of the many families to move into St. Lawrence County at the end of the Civil War were the members of what would become the Tompkins family of Canton.

Nancy Hayden[50] was born a slave in Virginia in June 1854. In about 1863, she came into the company of Martha Raymond, who brought her to live with her in Norwood. Martha Whalen Raymond was born in Canada in 1807. She married John Raymond in 1827. John was a first cousin of Benjamin Raymond, the founder of Potsdam. John and his brother Sewall were involved in many business deals with Benjamin Raymond.

John Raymond traveled extensively on business often, with Martha accompanying him. During the Civil War, after the Union captured New Bern, North Carolina, John Raymond spent many months in New Bern on business. The couple also traveled and lived in western New York near Chautauqua. They took up residence in Norwood in 1863.

Somewhere on these travels, the Raymonds met Nancy Hayden. The couple had only two children of their own, one of whom died as a young child. Perhaps this was why they took Nancy into their home.

Nancy was only nine years old when she arrived in Norwood. It is unclear whether she was ever taught to read and write; she is listed as illiterate on most census records throughout her life. This is ironic since just ten miles away in Madrid, the Scotch Presbyterian Church was actively raising funds and sending their members south to teach in freedom schools organized to educate newly freed slaves. Later reports mention that Nancy was very well mannered and dignified.

In February 1880, John Raymond died, and Martha Raymond became head of the household. Nancy Hayden continued to live in the Raymond household until 1884, as a servant. By then, Martha's health was failing, and she began to make plans to move to Chicago to live with her daughter. Martha Raymond died there of a stroke in 1885.

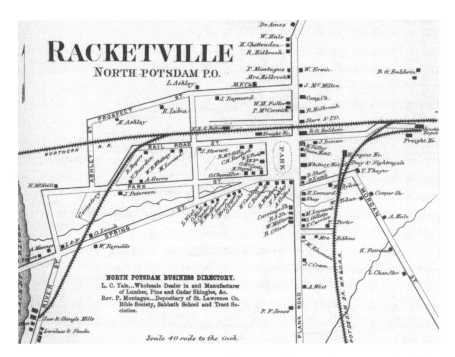

A map of Norwood (Racketville) showing the Raymonds' Prospect Street home. *From* New Topographical Atlas of St. Lawrence County from Actual Surveys by S.N. and D.G. Beers and Assistants *(1865; reprinted Churchville, NY: B and E Printers, Martin Wehle, 1976).*

Enter Walker Tompkins. Walker was born an enslaved person in the state of Virginia in March 1850. He became a camp follower during the Civil War and came back to the hamlet of Morley at the close of the war in 1865 with Rufus K. Jackson. Jackson was the county's military enrollment officer during the Civil War. He managed Harrison's Mills in Morley and was a county excise commissioner and surveyor.

By 1870, Walker had left the Jackson household and was living on the Thomas L. Harrison estate, attending school and working as a day laborer. Walker Tompkins would work for the Harrison estate for the next thirty years. Harrison, the son of one of the original proprietors of the town of Canton, was secretary of the New York State Agricultural Society and famous for his shorthorn cattle. In the 1870s, he sold one shorthorn cow for $6,000.

The Harrison estate was very well funded. In 1880, Walker Tompkins was one of five full-time servants of John A. Churchill, the overseer. The Harrison family funded the construction of the Morley Episcopal Church and the Gothic village schoolhouse. One of Walker's tasks included maintenance of the extensive estate gardens.

Walker Tompkins seemed to be accepted readily into the village social fabric, attending school and helping maintain the church grounds. He was even a member of the local unit of the Good Templars, an international temperance organization, participating in one of their public performances to favorable reviews.

He was encouraged to socialize and was introduced to Nancy Hayden in the early 1880s by some members of the community. Other Morley boys who were going courting in Norwood on a Saturday night would give him a ride so he could visit Nancy Hayden. With Martha Raymond about to break up household and move to her daughter's in Chicago, Walker Tompkins proposed to Nancy Hayden. They were married in 1884 at the Trinity Chapel in Morley.

They soon had two sons, both born in Morley: Franklin (known as Jake) Tompkins was born in June 1885 and Adelbert Tompkins on May 4, 1887. Both boys attended school in Morley and participated in local village affairs. Growing up on the banks of the Grasse River, Jake became a proficient fly fisherman. In later life, he would win a contest for longest cast at sixty-three feet. His fishing prowess was a thing of local legend.

The family remained in Morley until 1905, when they moved to 14 Pine Street in Canton. There, Walker and his two sons all worked as laborers. By

Morley's Gothic School, circa 1895. The two Black boys on the right are Franklin and Adelbert Tompkins. *St. Lawrence County Historical Association Archives, Canton, New York.*

Number 14 Pine Street, the Canton address where the Tompkins family lived from 1905 to 1915. *Photograph by Bryan Thompson.*

1910, Adelbert was splitting his time between Canton, where he is listed on the census as a stationary engine operator, and Norfolk, where he is listed as working in a paper mill. His Canton census record says he was literate, but the Norfolk census record lists him as illiterate. Both Jake and Walker were day laborers.

In 1914, Nancy was diagnosed with cancer. She died in Canton on June 28. Her funeral services were held in the Morley Trinity Church. An obituary was carried in the Canton *Plaindealer*, and a week later, Walker published a card of thanks to the people of Canton and Morley who had supported his family in their recent loss.[51]

Following Nancy Tompkins's death, Walker and Jake moved to a house on Dies Street in Canton. Adelbert Tompkins moved to Syracuse, where he registered for the draft on June 5, 1917. At the time, he was employed by the Semet-Solvay munitions factory. A year and one month later, on July 2, 1918, a massive explosion rocked Syracuse when a vat of TNT exploded, destroying the munitions factory and breaking windows for miles around. Dozens of employees were killed and others badly maimed. The trail of Adelbert goes cold from here. He is listed as dead in his father's obituary in 1927, but the family tombstone lists his death as 1932. No death is listed in the New York State death index for 1932.

Walker and Jake lived on Dies Street until 1927. Frank "Jake" purchased war bonds during World War I and trained to be a barber. He opened a barbershop in the Healey Block on Main Street in Canton. On January 31, 1927, a fire broke out in their home. The house was a total loss, but they were able to save their personal possessions with the help of neighbors.

The Tompkins pair moved to another rental property on Buck Street. On October 31, 1927, at 2:30 p.m., Walker Tompkins was walking across the railroad crossing on Buck Street, returning to work downtown after lunch. He was struck by a freight train, killing him instantly. He was laid to rest next to Nancy in the Morley churchyard. Newspaper accounts mention that he was affectionately called "our lazy n..r" by his friends, although he and his son were some of the hardest-working people in the community.

Jake the barber remained in Canton for the rest of his life. In 1930, he lost his lease on the shop in the Healey Block and moved his shop to Hodskin Street. His name appears often in the local press, associated with his prowess as a fisherman, throughout the 1930s.

In the 1930s, racial attitudes were darkening. In a newspaper column about Old Morley, Walker Tompkins is portrayed as Black people were portrayed in Hollywood movies of that period. He is portrayed as speaking pidgin English, simple-minded, unable to learn his lines for the play he had

Franklin "Jake" Tompkins departing on one of his famous fishing trips. *Courtesy of Canton Town Historian.*

appeared successfully in forty years before. The legend of the great squirrel hunt continued the stereotype. He was supposedly accidentally shot in the buttocks and just laughed it off, almost like he felt no pain—another common stereotype of Black people of the time.

Jake Tompkins himself came in for some of that stereotyping as well. A circus came to Canton in July 1937. The act included a bear. Larry Tobin, a local teller of tall tales, managed to spin some yarns around the bear and Jake. He convinced the Utica newspaper to write a story saying that Jake, a Black man, had wrestled the bear and bitten off its ear. A Rochester paper, not to be outdone, wrote that the bear had bitten off part of poor Jake's face. The *Ogdensburg Journal* said there was no wrestling at all; Jake had simply put a loose collar back on the bear. By the time Jake was interviewed by Canton's *Commercial Advertiser*, he claimed he knew nothing about any bear.

In January 1940, the local press reported on a poker game that was broken up at Frank Tompkins's Hodskin Street barbershop. It seemed that Jake had been allowing the men to play while they waited for their haircuts. They had been previously warned to stop the activity. The thirteen white men were arrested along with Jake.[52] The newspaper accounts made sure to point out that Jake was the only "negro" resident of Canton.

Just two weeks later, in February 1940, Jake was again arrested, this time for stealing firewood from the Maybee Coal Company yards. He spent the night in jail and was fined ten dollars. The *Advance-News* reported the incident, again accentuating the fact that he was the only Black man in town. The *Commercial Advertiser* went a step further in its racist reporting, referring to Tompkins as the "proverbial n****r in the woodpile."

After these two incidents, though Frank Tompkins continued to operate his barbershop, he disappears almost entirely from the press except for an obituary of an old fishing buddy and one other fishing reference. Frank Tompkins died in Canton in 1955 and is buried beside his parents in the Morley Cemetery.

## GEORGE B. SWAN AND EDWARD H. GREEN

The contrasting lives of two Black men, Edward Green and G.B. Swan, illustrate the changes in attitudes toward and evolving racial stereotypes of Black people in St. Lawrence County in the post–Civil War era.

## George B. Swan: "One of the Most Influential Citizens of Potsdam"

The story of George Swan is the exception to the common experience of Black pioneers in St. Lawrence County. Swan was born a free man on November 5, 1830, in Northfield, Franklin County, Massachusetts. He was the son of Calvin T. Swan and Rhoda Brown Swan, a mixed-race couple. His father was a carpenter.

Swan's namesake was his maternal uncle the Reverend George S. Brown. Brown was the first ordained Black Methodist minister in the eastern New York conference. When he preached in the Glens Falls area, no building was big enough to hold the crowd. Brown was an active abolitionist and a member of the American Colonization Society.[53] So George B. Swan was immersed in the spirit of abolitionism and racial self-worth from birth.

George B. Swan. *Courtesy of the Potsdam Museum, Potsdam, New York.*

By 1850, George Swan was living in Athol, Massachusetts, working as a tanner. He gradually began to accumulate wealth and business acumen. He moved first to the town of Hammond in St. Lawrence County, where he demonstrated his interest in politics, serving as a delegate to the Democratic (Free Soil) Party county convention in 1854.

Prior to 1860, he arrived in the village of Potsdam, where he returned to the familiar woodworking skills of his childhood and was working for the sash and door firm of Rich, Elderkin and Ellis. Within two years, he purchased an eighth interest in the business. At the time of the 1860 census, his occupation was master sash maker. While in 1850 he owned no property, by 1860, he owned $5,000 worth of real estate and $1,000 in personal property.[54]

In the spring of 1863, Swan was first elected trustee for the village of Potsdam.[55] The next year, Swan married Frances Newby, a white woman. Frances was the daughter of Robert and Ann Newby, who were English immigrants. The Newbys settled in the southern part of the town of Lisbon, in an area near Morley and Bucks Bridge, where one of the county's first abolitionist societies was organized in 1834.[56] The Newbys were active abolitionists.

George Swan's business career prospered during the Civil War. He obtained the contract to construct the army training camp Camp Union at

Potsdam. According to an article in the *Potsdam Herald*, "Swan spent extra care during the war tending to the families of his former employees who were serving in the war." His factory swelled to employ seventy-five to one hundred men.

In June 1868, he served on a St. Lawrence County Grand Jury. As the *Daily Journal* of Ogdensburg noted, he was only the second Black man in New York State to serve on a grand jury, Frederick Douglass of Rochester being the first. The article continued, "Mr. S. took an active part in the proceedings of that body, and a more energetic, faithful and conscientious man never entered the Grand jury rooms."[57]

Swan was an annual delegate representing Potsdam at the county Republican Party convention for over twenty years. In 1872, he was a county delegate at the New York State Republican Convention.[58] In addition to party politics, he was on the committee that established the first village of Potsdam public waterworks. G.B. Swan was a charter member of the Potsdam Fire Department and a member of the local Masonic Lodge.

His business interests continued to grow and prosper through the early 1870s despite some setbacks. His lumber-drying house burned in 1868 and again in 1871. On February 28, 1872, his carriage and general store burned to the ground. Each time, he rebuilt and expanded his operations.

In September 1873, economic panic hit the United States, slowing business everywhere. Construction activity ground to a halt across the country. The economic slowdown did not ease until 1879. G.B. Swan's businesses depended on house construction and were greatly impaired. He had to lay off most of his employees and take out numerous loans.

Despite the recession, he continued to run his various enterprises, including a farm. He was among the top prizewinners for his Ayrshire cattle at the 1876 Potsdam fair. He bred fine horses and sold a colt for $1,000. By 1880, Swan's business was improving. The *Ogdensburg Journal* of February 6, 1880, noted that Swan employed more men than he had in the previous three years.

Swan continued to be very active in public life. A local paper noted, "GB Swan of Potsdam is one of the most energetic Republicans. He has got 150 subscribers."[59] He was one of the local dignitaries noted as a guest at the 1881 Ogdensburg fair. He gave the speech at Mr. and Mrs. H.K. Burton's twentieth wedding anniversary and offered a toast at the Potsdam firemen's reunion. In September 1883, he was unanimously chosen chair of the St. Lawrence County Republican Convention.

Money and influence can affect how you are perceived. George B. Swan was a mixed-race man, yet in the 1850 and 1860 censuses, he was listed as

The 1870 U.S. Census, town of Potsdam, George Swan family. Showing change in racial status. *U.S. Census Bureau, HeritageQuest Online, New York State Library.*

white. As the racial prejudices and attitudes of the North changed following the Civil War, so did their concept of race. By 1870, Swan was listed initially as "mulatto," as was his daughter Jennie, while his wife was listed as white. At some point after the initial entry, Swan's designation was changed from "mulatto" to "white." His daughter's entry was left as "mulatto." By 1880, the issue of what race he was had become so important that he and his two children were bluntly listed as "mulatto."

By 1883, Swan owned the Parmeter Livery on Main Street; a second livery on Main Street; a double barn, an old livery and a blacksmith's shop on Swan Street; a sash and door factory as well as a store on Maple Street; and a planing mill on Fall Island.[60]

In the fall of 1883, many cases of typhoid fever were reported in the area. On December 8, the *Ogdensburg Journal* reported that G.B. Swan had been suffering from it. Swan remained ill and could not attend to his business throughout the winter.

On February 19, 1884, his eighteen-year-old daughter Jennie died. There was a huge outpouring of sympathy from the community. His workers, who numbered some forty people, marched at the front of the funeral procession. The noted local poet Helen Hinsdale Rich published a memorial poem to Jennie for Frances Swan. G.B. Swan was inconsolable and confined himself to his house.

About the same time, Swan was diagnosed with colon cancer. On April 14, 1884, he died at his home in Potsdam. His funeral was widely attended by people from across the county. His Masonic Lodge and the Potsdam Volunteer Fire Department attended in full regalia. His employees led the funeral procession. Every business in Potsdam was closed for his funeral.

G.B. Swan was remembered as a positive force in the community. His public spirit and zeal were always for the good of the town. His funeral was probably the largest ever held in St. Lawrence County for a Black man.

Swan had spent his life working for the betterment of Potsdam and his county through improving the public water supply, improving fire protection and helping those less fortunate than himself. He amassed a considerable fortune and had a street named for him. His estate inventory is over eight inches thick. Condolences to his family were published in the *New York Times* by the State Republican Party.

## Edward H. Green

He "had not the virtues which 'plead like angels trumpet tongued, against the deep damnation of his taking off,' yet many believe the verdict of the coroners jury was unjust, and that the man who 'snuffed him out' so unceremoniously should be punished."[61]

Edward Green was a Black man born in Windsor, Upper Canada, in about 1833. He came to the town of De Kalb in St. Lawrence County in the 1850s with his wife, Mary Bresset Green, a white woman, and her extended family. The Greens were tenants living in the Kendrew neighborhood of the town of De Kalb. Edward Green and his brothers-in-law Joseph and Stephen Bresset worked as laborers in the area.[62]

Mary Bresset Green died sometime in the mid-1860s. Her medical care left Edward in debt to Dr. William J.L. Millar. In January 1867, Millar was called on to care for Enos Potter Rice, who died on January 14, 1867. Millar wanted to perform an autopsy on Rice to study the congenital bone disease Rice suffered from. Why he did not consult Rice's family is unclear. Millar convinced Edward Green to assist him in exhuming the body of Rice to pay off Green's debt incurred for services rendered to the late Mary Bresset Green.

Millar and Green removed the body from the De Kalb Union Cemetery in the middle of the night. Green began to feel guilty and confessed the deed to friends of the Rice family. Legal authorities approached Millar's home, where they found him in the process of boiling body parts. According to a local press report, "The manner in which he commenced the work of dissection indicated that he knew nothing of anatomy or surgery, and very little of the butchering business."[63]

According to local news reports at the time, Green and Millar were arrested and placed in the county jail. Members of the local medical society immediately posted bail for Millar, who fled to Canada. Edward Green was quickly convicted of grave robbing in February 1867 and sentenced to six months in the Onondaga penitentiary.

Millar eventually returned to stand trial in the summer of 1867. His defense argued there was an error in the writ for his arrest and therefore the arrest was illegal. Through legal negotiations with the court, he eventually pleaded guilty. His sentence was a fine of $100. The editor of the *St. Lawrence Republican* noted the sentence and opined, "Allowing the Doctor's sentence to be a just one, in our opinion the accomplice should have gone free."[64]

Edward Green served his sentence and returned to De Kalb. In 1868, Green married another white woman named Mary. Their daughter Henrietta was born later that same year.

Green found it difficult to find outside work. He was growing a cash crop of hops on his land. Hop vines are traditionally grown on tall poles, and Green went into some neighboring undeveloped land, owned by absentee landlord Susan Danberry, to cut some saplings for poles. He was arrested and charged with larceny. He was convicted in December 1868 and sentenced to six months in the county jail.

This sentence seems quite harsh considering a similar charge was brought against a white man twenty-five years earlier in the same neighborhood for stealing many acres of oak trees from Danberry. In that case, the sentence was a fine of fifty dollars.

By 1870, Green was again living in the town of De Kalb, now on Maple Ridge Road. He leased $200 worth of real estate. He was living with his wife, Mary; Rhoda, his daughter by his first marriage; Henrietta, his daughter by his second marriage; and Emma Bresset, a relative of his first wife. Mary, another daughter, was born in 1871.

In about 1873, Green and his family moved to Champlain Street in Ogdensburg, where his second wife died. Green married his third wife, Marceline, a French Canadian woman, in about 1877. He and Marceline had a daughter, Rosianna, that year.

Green's rough reputation continued to make it difficult for him to find work. On October 25, 1878, he stole a heifer from Ann McGill in the town of Oswegatchie. He took it to Ogdensburg, where he sold the animal to the butcher Peter Kiah. The hide was sold to the local tannery. Ann McGill went to the tannery and recognized the hide of her missing heifer.

Green was tried in an unusual New Year's Day trial that lasted only three hours. On the same day, January 1, 1879, he was sentenced to five years in Clinton State Penitentiary. At the time of the 1880 U.S. Census, Green was living in that facility in Dannemora and two of his daughters, Hattie and Mary, were living in the Canton Village Children's Home.

After completing his sentence at Dannemora, Green returned to Ogdensburg. On May 8, 1885, he was observed assaulting his wife in the streets of Ogdensburg. He was charged and convicted of assault and battery in a Court of Special Sessions in Ogdensburg on May 12, 1885. He was sentenced to thirty days in the Onondaga County Penitentiary.[65] After his release in June, Green returned to his family on Champlain Street in Ogdensburg.

On Sunday, August 9, 1885, Edward, Marceline and Rosianna Green went fishing with a friend, Thomas Murphy, on the shore of the St. Lawrence River. Marceline had a pail for picking wild blackberries. Due to the erosion of the bank near a ravine on what is today the St. Lawrence Psychiatric Center grounds, the group climbed up the river embankment.

What happened next emerges in the coroner's inquest. In 1885, the land where the group arrived belonged to a market gardener, William B. Green, who made his living selling fruits and vegetables in Ogdensburg. W.B. Green had moved to the area from southern Ohio two years before. He was used to Black men being properly subservient.

Green had recently posted his land against trespassing. He came and warned the party away from his land. The various accounts differ, but it appears Edward Green argued that he had right of way on the riverbank of two or three rods by state law. A shouting match ensued.

W.B. Green went back to his barn, and Edward Green proceeded on the riverbank onto the lands of Hugh Lowry. W.B. Green returned to the riverbank with a hatchet and a cane and cursed and challenged Edward Green. Edward Green returned to the boundary of W.B. Green's property but, according to testimony, was still on Lowry's property by a few feet.

W.B. Green broke the cane over the head of Edward Green, who raised his hands in defense. W.B. Green then proceeded to sink the hatchet into Edward Green's chest, cutting a two-inch gash in his heart. Edward Green was standing downhill from his attacker and stumbled backward down the river embankment and soon died.

Edward Green's wife, Marceline, Hugh Lowry and Thomas Murphy all testified that Edward had a folded jackknife in his pocket when he died. Marceline took the knife from Edward Green's pocket. The placement of this knife would become increasingly significant as the case progressed.

W.B. Green immediately left the scene of the crime and proceeded to the home of attorney Daniel Magone, whom he secured as his attorney in the matter. Magone, in turn, secured the services of Dr. B.F. Sherman. They immediately went to the scene of the murder and removed the body, using two fence rails as a stretcher. After the body was removed, they sent William B. Green to contact local law enforcement officials.

The irascible Daniel Magone was no ordinary small-town lawyer. He was the best-known Democrat in all of northern New York. He had served as chair of the New York State Democratic Party in 1875 and 1876 and was a close associate of Governor Tilden. As such, Magone was involved in the national compromise of 1876, which allowed Rutherford B. Hayes to become president in exchange for the end of southern Reconstruction. Magone was an advocate for the Democratic Party's position of keeping "Negroes" in their place. In August 1886, President Grover Cleveland appointed him collector of the Port of New York.

A coroner's inquest was held three days after the murder, on August 1, 1885. Marceline Green was compelled to testify two hours before her husband's funeral. Edward Green's funeral procession passed by the hall as the coroner's jury was deliberating. The jury acquitted W.B. Green on grounds of self-defense since Edward Green was in possession of a jackknife.

Many people from the local press and area residents who knew the particulars of the case and the participants agreed with the sympathies of the local De Kalb reporter, who complained that Edward Green "had not the virtues which 'plead like angels trumpet tongued, against the deep damnation of his taking off,' yet many believe the verdict of the coroners jury was unjust, and that the man who 'snuffed him out' so unceremoniously should be punished."[66]

Eventually, a grand jury was impaneled in the case and an indictment of murder in the second degree was handed down against William B. Green. His trial began on May 10, 1886, in Canton, the county seat.

There are several firsthand newspaper accounts of the testimony, which vary in detailing the facts presented. Marceline Green and all others who spoke against the accused were subject to the type of character assassination typical of many defense teams. It seemed at times that the murder victim was on trial rather than the murderer himself. Marceline Green's testimony was attacked by revelations that she was in fact Edward Green's common-law wife of nine years. Her character was further smeared by references to the varied skin colors of her children fathered by Edward Green, implying they might have different fathers. When the widow Marceline Green tried to defend her character, "the court and council with the assistance of Crier Conkey, succeeded, after a hard struggle in shutting her off."[67]

Defense Attorney Magone in closing statements contrasted the witnesses for the prosecution with the "reputable" people called to testify for the defendant. "His invective when referring to the woman Marceline and the witness Crowley was bitter and scathing."[68]

In closing, County Prosecutor Lewis C. Lang discussed the particulars of the case. "He asked the jurors to discard any prejudice they might possibly have against the color of the deceased, urging that neither his color nor his previous character were to be considered as a justification of the taking of his life."[69] The jury deliberated for two and a half hours before finding the defendant not guilty.

Marceline Green attempted to enter a civil suit against William B. Green for the wrongful death of Edward Green. The proceeds from the suit were to be used for the support of Edward Green's minor children: Henrietta Green, Mary Green and Rosianna Green. There is no evidence the suit ever went forward.

If the story ended here, it would be a sad story of a poor man killed in a needless argument in front of his wife and child while fishing and berry picking. However, the story of Edward Green did not end in 1886.

Green's story, unlike the story of George B. Swan, would not go away. Swan's story—a Black man all of Potsdam honored at his death, a Black man with an estate inventory some eight inches thick—never graced the pages of the St. Lawrence County newspapers again after his death.

Racial attitudes in St. Lawrence County following the Civil War changed drastically. This can be seen in the language used by the local press in describing Black people. Before 1850, they were described as "colored," "the noble African," "slaves," "fugitives" and "bondsmen." The derogatory term "n****r" appears in print just twenty-nine times before 1850. Between 1850 and 1900, the same term appears in the local press more than two thousand times.

Before the Civil War, there were numerous interracial couples who, by all accounts, lived peacefully among their neighbors in the county. After the war, the local press was filled with reprinted articles condemning the practice.

In the 1870s and continuing into the 1890s, St. Lawrence County newspapers ran serial stories such as "A Lively Negro Wedding," "Glimpses of Dixie: The Broken Axle and the Smoking Car," "The Lime Kiln Club," "The Dakota Dialect," "The Tragedy of N****r Bend Camp" and many others. These stories introduced and reinforced stereotypes of the lazy, ignorant, criminal "Negro." All were written in pidgin English dialect.

The narrative of Edward Green fit right into these stereotypes. His story grew and grew as it was retold in the local press, beginning with two local newspapers in 1914. As it was retold, "N****r Green" became more and more horrible. The facts were rewritten so that he became "one of the worst desperadoes that ever dwelt within the county."[70]

This characterization would have surprised many local residents who had been around in 1867. In the same court term when Dr. Millar had been fined his $100 for grave robbing, the murder trial of Thomas Hand was held. In that case, Patrick Kennedy had traveled to St. Lawrence County from Canada to pose as the great-nephew of the hermit farmer Thomas Hand. He lived with the older gentleman until Hand revealed where he kept his gold in his house. Kennedy then pummeled the old man to death and stole his gold and his coat. In 1867, Patrick Kennedy was convicted of the brutal murder and hanged for the offense. Here was a true St. Lawrence County desperado in 1867!

Nonetheless, "N****r Green's" story was retold again in the spring of 1916 in four local newspapers. Now the desperado had robbed numerous local graves and was caught red-handed with a sack full of potatoes when he was murdered. In 1924, the story was retold three more times in local newspapers. This time, the horrible desperado Green was not only a grave robber but also a violent thief with superhuman strength who regularly robbed from the rich to aid the poor. In January 1945, the *Commercial Advertiser* (Canton) printed the story of the famous grave robber again. In 1948, the *Advance News* printed a final version of the story of the notorious snatching of bodies.

The story of "N****r Green," the grave robber, was still being retold in the neighborhood where Edward Green had lived in De Kalb as late as the 1990s. Few remembered or mentioned the role of Dr. William Millar in the case. Millar's sons attended St. Lawrence University and became prominent citizens, while Edward Green's children were not even allowed to attend the local common school.[71] Edward Green is buried in an unknown, unmarked grave in Ogdensburg. No death certificate was ever filed for him even though by 1886 New York State law required such a certificate to be filed for all persons who died in the state.

## Timeline, Chapter 4

| 1863 | Nancy Hayden arrives in Norwood with Martha Raymond. |
| --- | --- |
| 1863 | George B. Swan elected trustee of the village of Potsdam. |

| | |
|---|---|
| 1864 | George B. Swan marries Frances Newby. |
| 1865 April 9 | Confederate forces under General Robert E. Lee surrender at Appomattox, ending the Civil War. |
| 1865 April 14 | President Lincoln assassinated. Andrew Johnson sworn in as president. |
| 1865 July 2 | Charles Clarke arrives in St. Lawrence County. |
| 1865 December 6 | Thirteenth Amendment to the U.S. Constitution ratified. |
| 1865 | Walker Tomkins arrives in St. Lawrence County. |
| 1866 | Civil Rights Act passed over the veto of President Johnson. |
| 1867 January | Edward Green assists Dr. William Millar to exhume grave for autopsy. |
| 1867 February | Edward Green sentenced to six months for grave robbing. |
| 1867 July | Dr. William Millar fined $100 for grave robbing. |
| 1868 | Fourteenth Amendment to the U.S. Constitution ratified. |
| 1868 June | George B. Swan serves on county grand jury, second Black man to do so in New York State. |
| 1869 | Ulysses Grant sworn in as president. |
| 1872 | George B. Swan named St. Lawrence County delegate to state Republican convention. |
| 1873 | Edward Green moves to Ogdensburg. |

| | |
|---|---|
| 1877 | Compromise allows Rutherford Hayes to become president; in return, all troops are removed from old Confederacy, allowing the rise of Jim Crow. |
| 1877 | In *Hall v. DeCuir*, Supreme Court rules states cannot prohibit segregation on public transit. |
| 1881 | James Garfield sworn in as president. |
| 1881 | Chester Arthur sworn in as president following the assassination of Garfield. |
| 1883 | G.B. Swan chosen chair of St. Lawrence County Republican convention. |
| 1883 | Supreme Court rules Civil Rights Act of 1875 invalid. |
| 1884 April 14 | George B. Swan dies at Potsdam. |
| 1884 | Walker Tompkins marries Nancy Hayden. |
| 1885 | Grover Cleveland becomes president. |
| 1885 June | Franklin Tompkins born in Morley. |
| 1885 August 9 | Edward Green murdered by William B. Green. |
| 1886 May | William B. Green defended by Daniel Magone, is acquitted of murder. |
| 1886 August | Daniel Magone appointed collector for the Port of New York. |
| 1887 May | Adelbert Tompkins born in Morley. |
| 1889 | Benjamin Harrison sworn in as president. |

| | |
|---|---|
| 1893 | Grover Cleveland sworn in for second term. |
| 1896 May 18 | In *Plessy v. Ferguson*, Supreme Court upholds separate but equal, cementing Jim Crow laws. |
| 1897 | William McKinley sworn in as president. |
| 1905 | Tompkins family move to Pine Street in Canton. |
| 1914 June 28 | Nancy Tompkins dies. |
| 1924 January | Charles Clarke committed to county poorhouse. |
| 1926 March 26 | Charles Clarke dies. |
| 1927 October 31 | Walker Tompkins hit by train and dies. |
| 1955 | Franklin "Jake" Tompkins dies at Canton nursing home. |

## CHAPTER 5

# THE INDUSTRIAL ERA AND THE DECLINE OF THE BLACK COMMUNITY (1900–1930)

I n the early twentieth century, a new national racist compact was emerging, with the full flowering of Jim Crow in the South. The erasure of George B. Swan's legacy as a businessman and civic leader; the lack of justice for the murder of Edward Green compounded by ongoing racist stereotypes of his life; Charles Clark's lonely last years lived in a barn and then in the St. Lawrence County Poorhouse: all illustrate a downward spiral in racial attitudes toward Black people locally. A type of shared, willful community amnesia helped to erase the memory of numerous other St. Lawrence County Black pioneers between 1900 and 1930. Local attitudes adjusted themselves to a national trend toward acceptance of racial inequality and injustice.

Black civil rights took yet another disastrous blow when Woodrow Wilson was elected president in 1912, filling his cabinet with southern segregationists and allowing cabinet members to introduce racial segregation to their departments. The Department of the Navy, which had not been segregated since the War of 1812, now allowed Black sailors to serve only as cooks and scullery help. At the same time, new industrial jobs in northern factories, especially when war broke out in Europe in 1914, encouraged the Great Migration out of the South.

The Black population of St. Lawrence County, being mostly landless, had always been quite mobile, moving from town to town wherever there was ready employment. The population had been spread out through several towns. By the beginning of the twentieth century, however, larger factories were being located in Ogdensburg and Massena, and the Black population was centered there, influenced by industrial developments.

The Aluminum Company of America (ALCOA) opened its first plant in Massena in 1903. The ALCOA monopoly was controlled by the industrialist Andrew Mellon.[72] In August 1915, a bitter five-day strike occurred at the Massena plant when workers discovered that ALCOA was paying them $1.65 per day while workers at a similar ALCOA plant in Niagara Falls earned $2.25 per day. Over two thousand workers went out on strike. Three companies of the New York State Militia were called out to subdue the strikers who had taken over the Massena plant.[73] At least one worker was killed and another deported for organizing the strike. In total, thirteen strikers were arrested. On August 4, the *New York Times* reported that ALCOA was importing strikebreakers from distant points.

"With Mellon interests came the Frick[74] model of labor relations, which used ethnic divisions to strip workers of power."[75] In Massena as elsewhere in the country, stoking ethnic tensions involved recruiting Black workers as well as immigrant labor.

For example, one of the worst race riots in American history, in East St. Louis, Illinois, in 1917, started outside an aluminum facility, as white workers on strike faced 470 Black strikebreakers recruited from the South. The local authorities stood aside as white mobs murdered over 200 African Americans.[76] ALCOA used similar tactics in Massena to limit labor organization, even as the tactics endangered Black lives.

At the time of the 1915 New York State Census for Massena, 24 percent of the population of Massena was listed as alien. Just five Black people in the town were listed. Two were laborers, one was a chef, one was a dress maker and one was a housewife. In early 1915, there were no Black workers at ALCOA in Massena. After the 1915 strike, the Industrial Workers of the World (IWW) labor organization was actively trying to organize the plant. In response, plant management started to bring in Black workers in late 1915. They created temporary housing for the new Black employees in the idle Fiber Plant building at the corner of Park Avenue and Willow Street.

These employees reached St. Lawrence County just before D.W. Griffith's film *The Birth of a Nation* played in county theaters in the spring of 1916. The movie positively portrayed the southern narrative of the lost cause: a belief in the benignity of slavery, the horrid corruption of Reconstruction and the noble role of the Ku Klux Klan in restoring proper racial order to society. The editor of the *Madrid Herald* was typical in heaping ecstatic praise on the film after viewing it in Potsdam on May 5. He stated:

*Especially Northern young people need to see* [the film]….*Another great lesson may well be learned in the revengeful policy of the North in making the ignorant negro a citizen, for evolution—God's plan of growth by related steps cannot be disregarded without incurring disaster. Had North and South been willing to use one tenth of the cost of the war in teaching and segregating the Negro, the war itself would never have been fought…and the damning chapters of race problem never would have been written.*[77]

Even as *The Birth of a Nation* spread negative images of Black people, ALCOA was recruiting them at rates as high as two hundred per week. ALCOA was a paternalistic employer seeking to keep a ready workforce and crush dissent through meeting its employees' needs cradle to grave. The company started the Pine Grove housing development in Massena in 1907 to meet the rapidly expanding housing requirements of its employees. Pine Grove would grow to include individual houses of several styles, as well as segregated rooming houses and clubhouses for white and colored workers, introducing southern Jim Crow standards to their operation. A community playground was included in the development. The last Pine Grove house was sold in 1952. Easy purchase terms were offered to ALCOA employees with payments deducted directly from paychecks. The company even had its own hospital and milk station where employees could get safe pasteurized milk.

Temporary worker housing at Massena. *St. Lawrence County Historical Association Archives, Canton, New York.*

Demand for aluminum soared as World War I raged in Europe. The Massena workforce would eventually balloon to three thousand workers in 1919. To meet the constant demand for worker housing, ALCOA built four residential hotels to house workers: Hatfield House, DeGrasse Hotel, Lincoln Hotel (exclusively for colored workers) and Poplar Hotel.

Starting in 1917, many ALCOA workers were being drafted into the armed forces. This included Black employees. Curtis Sneed was one of these Black draftees. He was awarded the Croix de Guerre by the French government. He returned to his job on the potline at Massena following the cessation of hostilities.

Curtis Sneed. *Aluminum Bulletin*, September 1919. *St. Lawrence County Historical Association Archives, Canton, New York.*

Despite the need for Black workers and their service in World War I, local racist attitudes associated Black people with crime. On October 3, 1917, twenty-two-year-old Bessie White was tragically murdered on the grounds of the new high school in downtown Massena. The only evidence at the scene was a red handkerchief. Despite the lack of evidence, all the local papers reported, "A quiet search is being conducted among the employees of the Aluminum Company of America. The company has imported a number of laborers of a very low scale and it is believed that the crime was committed by one of these. Of this number about 200 are negroes and others are recruited from the lowest stratum of society."[78] Coverage in the *New York Times* was much different. It did not mention race and said the crime remained a mystery. Massena offered a $500 reward for evidence leading to an arrest. Three different Black men, two from Syracuse and one from Ohio, were arrested and released. Every Black employee at ALCOA was interrogated with no breakthroughs.

The murder of Bessie White was never solved. The handling of the case has chilling parallels to how the case of blood libel, the Jewish community and Barbara Griffith was handled by Massena authorities just a decade later, allowing local prejudice to overrule evidence and common sense (for more on this case, see pages 101–2). In the White case, large amounts of time were wasted interviewing Black workers owing to local prejudice rather than looking more widely in the community for a suspect. The blood libel case has been widely discussed in several books.[79]

Despite these challenges, the *Aluminum Bulletin*, an ALCOA newsletter begun in March 1918, shows the development of a Black community. The *Aluminum Bulletin* regularly ran columns on worker safety, community events and items for the promotion of the public good. The newsletter went to great lengths to cover activities by all its various employee groups, advertising English language classes, public performances in Hungarian, local sports teams and more.

In August 1918, the bulletin reported that Mrs. L.E. Hopson of 88 Chase Street was seeking subscribers for the *Chicago Defender*. She was the local reporter for the newspaper and solicited news items from among the Black ALCOA employees for a Massena column she would author. The *Defender* was one of the most influential Black newspapers of the era. Its pages encouraged the Great Migration and challenged Jim Crow rules throughout the nation.

The first Massena news article appeared in the *Defender* on August 9, 1918. Titled "Southern Tactics in Massena," the article tells a chilling tale of how Judge Giles A. Chase ran his local court. When sentencing a Black couple, he was alleged to have said, "'You may be a smart [n****r], but we don't want any [n*****rs] in this town anyway. And I am going to fix you so you will never do any more business in this state.' It is said that Judge Chase makes this same remark to every Race man[80] who comes before him."[81] The article went on to claim that white witnesses had come forward to say Judge Chase offered to lower their sentences for intoxication if they implicated certain Black businessmen.

The article further stated that the plaintiffs in this affair had filed a complaint of judicial misconduct with New York State governor Whitman, whose office had acknowledged the complaint. There is no record of any action being taken against Judge Chase, who would remain in office in Massena until 1927, sentencing multiple Black people to banishment.

The article also described an earlier incident: "On July 18th [1918], fifteen Race men arrested, charged with gambling and, without further ado, Judge Chase sentenced the men to from five to twenty five days a piece without allowing them any chance to speak for themselves."[82] No local press covered these arrests. The local court dockets have not survived to confirm or deny these arrests.

The same month, the *Aluminum Bulletin* portrayed a different picture, one of community building.[83] The Reverend Eli K. Harris of the pot rooms had commenced regular Sunday services for Black workers at 7:30 p.m. in the ALCOA gymnasium. By February 1919, Reverend Harris had moved his services to the upper floor of the Pine Grove Realty Company. His wife,

## A Firm Believer in Safety

Do you know who this man is ?

Take a good look at him, and when you see him in the plant ask him what he thinks of Safety.

Tom Bowleg is employed as a tapper in building 14, potroom. Last fall he burned the sole of his right foot. He was wearing poor shoes at the time. He now wears good shoes, and also believes in protecting the windows of his soul, his eyes.

One look at the picture will show where the hot metal splashed against his goggles. Without those goggles, Tom would be a blind man, today. No one knows it any better than he does. When he was asked if he didn't want to say something about it for the benefit of the boys to help them to protect themselves from injury and pain, Tom said, "Be Careful." Boys! he said a mouthful.

Get used to your goggles and you will find yourself thankful many times that you protected your eyes.

If the men in the plant could only see some of the eye-burns which come up to the hospital for treatment, they would pause a second time before leaving off the goggles. Nearly all eye-burn cases have to be laid off for a time to prevent infection, and possibly loss of sight.

As the owl says, "BE WISE!"

Safety first: *Aluminum Bulletin*, March 1920. *St. Lawrence County Historical Association Archives, Canton, New York.*

Winifred Harris, led the Sunday school classes from there and later from their home. The piece ended with the note, "All you colored gentlemen should see Rev. Harris."[84]

By 1920, the plant employed as many as thirty-seven Black men in its foundry or pot rooms. Of the Black workers at ALCOA, 95 percent worked in the pot rooms, which were especially dangerous, with more worker turnover than in any jobs in the factory. In the ALCOA insurance claims published in the local paper, there are more for pot room injuries than in any other branch of the factory.

Jack Clendenen, a 1914 pot room employee, wrote the following ditty about the work:

*In June, July, and August, when the sun is bright and hot,*
*Just get a job in the pot rooms, a-breaking in a pot.*
*You will find there many people of different tribes and lots:*
*They all will mingle together, a-breaking in the pots.*
*When you think your back's most broken on crusts much harder than rocks.*
*The lights start out, ten at a crack—when you're breaking in the pots.*
*You start to tap; the pots are cold the bath is nice and hot.*
*You'll find good sport in the pot rooms, a breaking in the pots.*[85]

By 1920, local papers were referring to what they called the "colored section" of Massena. The colored section in the Pine Grove centered around Canal Street (today Jefferson Avenue) and Railroad Avenue (today Liberty Avenue) and the side streets immediately connecting to Railroad Avenue.

This larger Black community faced new realities. Following the end of World War I, demand for aluminum declined. The recession of 1921 saw the company stop all construction of new housing at the Pine Grove development. However, it did not stop recruiting Black men to work in the plant. A number of newly hired Black families moved into houses along Canal Street.

ALCOA continued to print the *Aluminum Bulletin* until the end of 1920. The loss of the newsletter was a big blow to the fledgling Black community. They lost the one positive voice covering the local Black community. Marriages and other social events in the Black community such as the marriage of James W. Holmes and Junia Winbush in May 1919[86] went unpublished in the local press. So did birthday and graduation celebrations. Only criminal acts as defined by Judge Chase were fodder, each perpetrator highlighted by announcement of their race.

Single Black women were especially vulnerable to charges of prostitution. In May 1923, Judge Chase dealt with three Black women so charged. Each in turn was fined fifty dollars and told to be on the next train out of Massena or spend three months in jail. One woman was also warned to never return. Two other Black women who had been renting rooms in the same house were charged with the misdemeanor of living in a disorderly house and told to be on the 6:10 p.m. train out of town. Like most of the accused from the Black community before them, none of the women asked for a jury trial. The two white men who testified against the women were let off with a warning.

One particularly detailed case of attacks on Black women involved Maggie White. When ALCOA opened the Lincoln Hotel, the firm hired Lovick and Maggie White to run the place. Lovick White, born in Georgia

2238          LINCOLN HOTEL (For Colored Men)          5-15-20

*Aluminum Bulletin,* October 1920. *St. Lawrence County Historical Association Archives, Canton, New York.*

in 1898, was one of the many Black men recruited by ALCOA during World War I. He registered for the draft in Massena in September 1918. All seemed to go well. The hotel was usually at capacity. The ALCOA hotels provided a cafeteria for resident and visitor meals and laundry and cleaning services for all the residents. Evening entertainment was sometimes provided in the dining room.

The Whites had an assistant manager, Daniel McDow, also Black. There was a constant turnover of kitchen and maid staff. In the spring of 1923, Maggie White traveled to Tennessee, where she hired three Black women to work in the Lincoln Hotel. On August 15, 1923, officers conducted a midnight raid on the hotel where they reported finding fifty Black people, including several women. Searching the people and premises, the officers found three and three-quarters quarts of Old Crow whiskey, half a pint of whiskey in a flask and a quart and a half of undetermined alcohol. Lovick White was indicted and sent to federal jail in Utica.

The following Saturday, Maggie White was arrested and charged with keeping a disorderly house at the Lincoln Hotel. Once again, having single Black women in your employ could mean only one thing: prostitution. But here is where the story diverges from what had become normal procedures in Judge Chase's courtroom. Maggie White had the audacity to demand a jury trial. The case against her and the three women was dismissed for lack of evidence. Nonetheless, the local police and judiciary would continue to harass Maggie White for four years until they finally forced her to leave Massena.

In October 1923, another incident led to the following report: "Feelings over the crime ran high Sunday morning and fearing that a lynching would be attempted Chief of Police Demo…hustled Williams to the Police Station where he was speedily arraigned."[87]

An itinerant Black man, who was not a part of the Massena Black community, in a drunken spree allegedly had wounded two people and kidnapped and raped a local native woman. The newspaper in bringing up the idea of a lynching was almost calling certain elements to action.

The local press used multiple means to show the local Black community in a most unfavorable light. The papers even advertised a local debate, the topic of which was "The American Negro as a national asset or liability."[88] When articles demeaning Black people were printed, they often were highlighted or printed in bold. An example, from the *Norwood News* of March 23, 1921, is shown below.

In the same years, ALCOA continued to support and recruit Black workers. Black couples such as James and Anna Sims moved their whole family, including seven children, from New York City to Massena. James got a job as a pot man at ALCOA. Soon after, their oldest son, Milton Simms, joined his father at the mill. Their last child, Rudolph Valentino Simms, was born in Massena on July 3, 1926. He was named for the famed Italian silent movie star and heartthrob who died of a ruptured ulcer six weeks later, at age thirty-one. "Rudy" Sims would go on to be a track star for the New York University School of Commerce.

By 1920, the ALCOA baseball league had a Black team, the Colored Giants. The team played exhibition games against local teams in St. Lawrence County.[89] Its origins go back to July 1917, when ALCOA hired Alexander Ellerby to work in the factory. He was a former Negro League baseball player. He soon ran three rooming houses, mostly

**Discovered She Had Negro Blood, Now Seeks Divorce**

Mrs. Mary LeFevre of San Francisco, strikingly beautiful and possessor of charming old South manners, said in her petition for divorce, filed recently, that two years after her marriage to Frederick LeFevre, Louisiana planter, she discovered there was negro blood in her veins. This, she felt, was an insurmountable barrier, for her pride equaled that of her husband's for his family name. She said her husband pleaded with her to forget it, but this she is unable to do, after consulting scientists, who said the negro strain might come to the surface generations ahead.

*Norwood News*, March 23, 1921.
*New York State Historic Newspapers.*

Rudy Sims wins a race. *NYU School of Commerce Yearbook, 1942.*

catering to Black employees of ALCOA. He was also a musician and formed a local "colored" orchestra that played at dances in the area. He was famous for his love of baseball and putting on a good show. The *Observer* noted, "He always furnished great sport at every game he attended. In the days when he was manager of the colored team, fans had the greatest fun with him. 'Pull him out.' They would yell at Ellerby when some dusky player would make a bad play. It did not matter whether the play was trivial or serious. Ellerby would always pull the man out if the fans said so."[90]

Native-born white Massena locals enjoyed a cultural life enriched by their Black and immigrant residents. But these same locals were shaped by nativist and racist organizing in the 1920s. The Johnson-Reed Act was signed into law on May 26, 1924, severely limiting the number of foreign workers allowed into the country. In exception to the act, in October 1924, the *New York Times* reported that Secretary of the Treasury Andrew Mellon's ALCOA organization had a special agreement with the Ogdensburg immigration office to import foreign workers through Canada. The permits were generally for one to three hundred foreigners as occasion demanded.[91] Mellon could import foreign workers even after the border was closed.

Immigrants, African Americans, Jews and Catholics were targets of the Ku Klux Klan (KKK) in the 1920s. To understand how race relations changed in St. Lawrence County in the second decade of the twentieth century, we need to understand how the KKK rose to prominence and influenced public opinion in the area.

The second KKK was set up as a pyramid scheme wherein the Klan kleagle (recruiter) kept a portion ($2 or $3) of the $10 membership fee of each member he signed up. (The fee in today's currency would amount to $140.) Each member who brought in a new recruit got $1 of the membership fee.

By late 1922, the Klan had a kleagle for northern New York in Watertown (Jefferson County). In December of that year, the *Republican Journal* of

*Right*: The Sycamore Street rooming house run by A. Ellerby. *Photograph by Bryan Thompson.*

*Below*: *Aluminum Bulletin*, October 1920. *St. Lawrence County Historical Association Archives, Canton, New York.*

COLORED GIANTS BASEBALL TEAM

Ogdensburg reported that the Klan had mailed letters throughout northern New York. Each letter included a questionnaire to determine eligibility.[92] As stated in the entrance requirements to a Klan rally in Prescott, Ontario, a few years later, "only white, gentile, protestants will be admitted."[93] The twenty questions asked for reasons for wanting to join, religious affiliation, nationality, politics, church membership, fraternal order membership, physical description and belief in white Protestant supremacy and pure Americanism.

Two weeks before this local membership drive, on December 2, 1922, the Reverend A.H. McKnight, Baptist minister of Potsdam, gave a sermon on the KKK. He

There will be dances given at the

**Pine Grove Hall**

Beginning Friday evening, March 14. Thursday afternoons, 2:30 to 4:30 free. Tuesday, Thursday and Friday evenings, from 8:00 p. m., price 55c. Ladies, 35c.

EVERY ONE IS WELCOME

Given by

**A. L. ELLERBY**

Mgr. of Colored Giants

Colored orchestra will furnish music later on

*Massena Courier*, March 6, 1924. *New York State Historic Newspapers.*

spoke largely in support of the organization, claiming its goals as noble. "We are told the Klan will not receive Jews, Catholics, Negroes or foreigners. Is that anything serious?" he preached. He did, however, condemn the organization for secrecy as an element not conducive to democracy.[94]

The Klan's activities in the county led to much dissension in local churches and fraternal organizations. The state Masons organization came out firmly against any affiliation with the group, yet the De Peyster lodge allowed Klan rallies to be held in its hall. The Grand Lodge of the Independent Order of Odd Fellows (IOOF) refused to take a position. The Northern New York Presbytery came out in opposition to the Klan, yet a Reverend Lacey who spoke at Klan rallies in the county was a member of that denomination. The Northern New York Conference of the Methodist Church would not allow KKK representatives to speak at its conference meetings. In January 1927, the leaders of the conference went out of their way to let the public know that fewer than a dozen of their ministers were members of the Klan.[95] Yet several of their ministers, including the Reverend Ralph Stevens of the town of Macomb, served as chaplains for local KKK chapters. The Reverend W.O. Hull of Hammond gave sermons in support of the Klan.

Nationally, by 1923 the Klan was getting increasingly bad press, but that did not seem to hurt local recruitment in St. Lawrence County. The Klan sent the Reverend W. Jeffries Whaley, a Southern Methodist minister, to

Watertown as the new kleagle for northern New York. Accompanied by his bodyguard, he launched an aggressive membership campaign that would net the organization thousands of local members.

The following chart lists dates and places of known St. Lawrence County Klan rallies over the next six years.

| Date | Location | Attendance (if known) |
| --- | --- | --- |
| November 1923 | Benson Mines | |
| November 1923 | Edwards | |
| December 10, 1923 | Thompson Park, Watertown | |
| October 31, 1924 | Hammond | |
| December 1924 | Gouverneur Mailing | |
| May 5, 1925 | De Kalb, Ideauma Road | |
| May 12, 1925 | De Peyster | |
| May 19, 1925 | De Peyster | |
| June 15, 1925 | Hermon | |
| August 25, 1925 | Potsdam | |
| September 2, 1925 | Pitcairn Forks | |
| October 25, 1925 | Pitcairn Forks | |
| May 5, 1926 | South Russell | |
| June 1, 1926 | Hailesboro | |
| June 2, 1926 | Fowler, Love Farm | 3,000 |
| June 6, 1926 | Fowler, Woodcock's | |
| July 27, 1926 | Gouverneur | |
| August 1926 | Morristown | 5,000 |
| August 4, 1926 | Russell Town Hall | |
| August 4, 1926 | Basie Corners Methodist Church | |
| August 25, 1926 | Pitcairn/Harrisville | 3,000 |
| September 1926 | Fowler, Love Farm | |
| September 14, 1926 | Pierce's Corners | |

| Date | Location | Attendance (if known) |
|------|----------|----------------------|
| September 21, 1926 | Woodbridge Corners | |
| November 9, 1926 | De Peyster Odd Fellows/Masonic Lodge | |
| May 20, 1927 | Potsdam IOOF Lodge | |
| June 1, 1927 | Massena Town Hall | |
| June 18, 1927 | Potsdam, Norwood Road | |
| June 24, 1927 | Waddington Pine Grove | |
| June 24, 1927 | Massena | |
| July 1927 | Parishville Town Hall | |
| July 9, 1927 | Brier Hill | |
| July 22, 1927 | Macomb/Pleasant Lake | |
| July 23, 1927 | Potsdam, Norwood Road | 5,000 |
| July 31, 1927 | Louisville/Mack Island | |
| August 8, 1927 | Parishville | |
| August 19, 1927 | Heuvelton/Ridge Hill | |
| September 20, 1927 | Gouverneur, Richville Road | |
| September 25, 1927 | Potsdam, Norwood Road | |
| October 22, 1927 | Lisbon Town Hall | |
| November 2, 1927 | West Stockholm | Attend chicken pie supper |
| July 1, 1928 | Heuvelton Hall | |
| July 11, 1928 | Potsdam, Norwood Road | |
| September 1, 1928 | Macomb | |
| July 11, 1929 | Potsdam, Norwood Road | |

In November 1924, two crosses were burned inside the village limits of Hammond. The editor of the *Hammond Advertiser* was careful to stay neutral in the debate, stating that it was nobody else's business what clubs an individual chose to join. Yet this editor was the only one in St. Lawrence County who named the names of some of the participants in the KKK activities. Other than that, from the outset the local press never mentioned the names of the Klan's victims or perpetrators, even as the Klan became increasingly vocal and vindictive. In Watertown, Charles Lee, publisher at the Hungerford-Holbrook Printing Company, refused to print Klan literature. As a warning, he was publicly blacklisted by the Klan.[96]

The May 14, 1925 *Ogdensburg Journal* reported, "A determined campaign to proselytize St. Lawrence County and place thousands of its residents under the banner of the Invisible Empire is now underway by the Ku Klux Klan."[97] Up until this time, all the publicized rallies had been in the western portion of St. Lawrence County, closer to the kleagle's headquarters in Watertown. The first KKK rally in the eastern portion of the county occurred in August 1925 in Potsdam.

On June 21 of that year, a cross was burned on the railroad right-of-way near Hammond. The *Hammond Advertiser* suggested the burning might have been the work of "errant boys."

The September 1926 rally on the Love Farm in Fowler was attended by the Reverend William J. M'Cullough of the Gouverneur Baptist Church. The following week, M'Cullough gave an eloquent sermon published in many local newspapers about the great works of the Ku Klux Klan. He allowed for the Klan's weaknesses by stating, "No organization, not even the church can be too seriously condemned because of certain of its members. The spirit and the program are the important issues."[98]

The Klan, however, did much more than hold rallies. In June 1925, the Klan forced Charles B. Smith to remove flags from his golf course near Morristown. Exactly why is unclear. They continued to send letters to targeted citizens throughout the county, suggesting they leave town. It soon surfaced that several residents of Heuvelton, including a decorated World War I veteran, also received letters. The veteran publicly notified the Klan to come and get him. Again, all victims' names were suppressed. St. Lawrence County district attorney William Ingram was called to investigate the use of the U.S. mail to send threats.

In a particularly onerous case, in Natural Dam (town of Gouverneur), a hooded Klan member knocked on the door of a decorated Word War I veteran at 10:00 p.m., demanding that he leave town within twenty-four hours because he was Canadian (and perhaps Catholic).[99] The newspaper gave all the details of his service. The family took the threat seriously and left town, but local newspapers continued not to divulge any of the names of those driven out by the Klan. The same paper gave full gory details when a man was crushed to death by a falling safe but would not give the pertinent details about a Klan victim.

Early in 1926, a group of hooded Klansmen surrounded county DA Ingram as he left his office in Canton. They demanded that he remove all Catholic employees from his office and pledge to never hire another. Ingram refused.[100]

St. Lawrence County assistant district attorney Andrew J. Hanmer, of Massena, who had tried most of the county cases against Black defendants in Massena, agreed to the Klan's terms and became their candidate for the DA office in the Republican primary. There ensued a very acrimonious battle for the Republican nomination. The Republican establishment rallied their supporters for a door-to-door campaign for Ingram. It was a very tight race. The city of Ogdensburg and the town of Gouverneur went overwhelmingly for Ingram. Most of the towns in the eastern part of the county, where the Klan had not been active, supported Hanmer, the Klan candidate, while the towns in the western, Klan-riddled part of the county largely rejected him. Overall, the primary was a rebuke of the rising power of the Klan and their methods in St. Lawrence County.[101]

While the election was a rebuke for the Klan, the campaign had no ill effect on Hanmer's career. He remained deputy district attorney. When Ingram advanced to county judge, Hanmer became the new county DA. When Ingram died in 1937, Hanmer succeeded him as county judge. In 1930s St. Lawrence County, KKK affiliation seemed to be a career asset.

A large number of Klan rallies were held in the Massena area. In 1927, the Massena Town Hall hosted one of them. C.B. Smith, the New York State grand dragon, spoke at several of these meetings. Crosses were

## SMASHING VICTORY FOR INGRAM AT THE PRIMARY TUESDAY

Carries County by Majorities Ranging From 1,500 to 1,700—The Ku Klux Klan Opposed the Candidacy of Mr. Ingram—Gouverneur and Potsdam Went Big for Mr. Ingram—Hanmer Carries Massena.

*Northern Tribune,* September 15, 1926. *New York State Historic Newspapers.*

Andrew J. Hanmer, deputy district attorney. *St. Lawrence County Courthouse.*

burned and intimidating letters continued to circulate. Both Potsdam Klavern #208 and Massena's Power City Klavern #212 were chartered in 1927, when at least ten KKK rallies are known to have been held in the Potsdam/Massena area. A cross was burned behind Kauffman's store on Main Street in Massena. The Massena Klan even rented their own meeting hall at 124 Maple Street.

One of the most dramatic examples of anti-Semitism in the nation occurred in the context of Klan activism in St. Lawrence County. On September 22, 1928, a four-year-old girl, Barbara Griffith, disappeared from the village of Massena. In December, Mary Church Terrell, reporting for the Black *Chicago Defender*, described the incident most eloquently:

*A striking exhibition of the length to which some people will go who are filled with race prejudice was recently given in a New York town. This time the Jews were the victims. Two days before Yom Kippur, their great day of atonement, a child 4 years old suddenly disappeared. The mayor of Massena immediately summoned a rabbi and questioned him closely about the little girl. There is a myth that the Jews offer the blood of children in certain service connected with their day of atonement and there was a decided tendency to connect the child's disappearance with this. In other words, the rabbi might have been charged with murder. Fortunately, the little girl was found wandering in the woods nearby. But the Jews did not allow this outrage to slip by without a loud and indignant protest.*

*They called upon the governor of the great state of New York to investigate the matter and take some action. He did and the corporal of the state guard who brought the rabbi before the town authorities to be questioned by them was immediately suspended. But the Jews were not satisfied with that. They insisted the mayor be dealt with. Governor Smith did not have the power to remove that interrogative gentleman who had been elected by the people, but he suggested, no doubt, that it would be wise for that official to say a word or two himself just at that juncture. The mayor then took his pen in hand and wrote a letter of abject apology for summoning the rabbi to explain the disappearance of the child. "I am confirmed in my opinion," he said, "that I have committed a serious error of judgement into which I was led by excitement. I feel I ought to express my deep and sincere regret that I should have seemed to lend countenance to what I have known was a cruel libel."*

*And that is just the point of the whole thing. People who are filled with prejudice against others who differ from them either in race, or religion have no judgement at all. They believe anything they hear about victims of their hatred and contempt. The actions taken by the Jews in New York is a good example for every maligned group to follow.*[102]

The local press stopped reporting on local Klan activities in their pages after listing one last large meeting planned for the hill just outside Norwood on July 11, 1929. The incident at Massena and the Supreme Court ruling supporting the Walker Act had taken their toll.

During the 1920s, some people did speak out. The Reverend Harry Adams Hersey of the Canton Universalist Church published an article in a Universalist publication in which he discussed his experiences living in Indiana under severe Klan influence. He described the Klan as "fraught with danger" for the communities where it took root.[103]

William F. Anderson, who used his ads in the *Courier and Freeman* of Potsdam to comment on local affairs, was almost a lone voice as he repeatedly passed wry comments on the Klan in his ads. His criticisms did not seem to hurt his business, as he continued to advertise his red cedar shingles at ninety cents a bundle on a weekly basis.

The 1920s were a fraught decade for America's Black citizens. The pseudo-science of the 1925 Army War College Report on "The Use of Negro Manpower in War" was seized upon by middle-class white Americans to exclude Black people from all manner of skilled occupations and education.

At the beginning of the 1920s, there was a stable population of around 150 Black people in St. Lawrence County. By 1930, the population had dropped by two-thirds to fewer than 50 individuals. At a talk in the Edwards Public Library in 2008, I was displaying a graph showing this dramatic drop when a nonagenarian in the audience, Donald Mac Gregor, stood up and said, "I can tell you what happened to the Black people. It was the men in the white sheets."

As they had with Klan activities, the local press never divulged who the local Klan members were. They also never covered the local Black community unless there was some kind of run-in with the law. In May 1923, the *Massena Observer* noted, "The court room was a mighty dark

Number 124 Maple Street, headquarters of the KKK in Massena. *Photo by Bryan Thompson, September 2022.*

place Tuesday morning, there being several colored witnesses."[104] In the nineteenth century, various interracial couples like George and Francis Swan of Potsdam lived harmoniously in their communities. After 1920, none appear on local censuses.

# K. K. K.

P. T. Barnum said years ago that there was a sucker born every minute, and Abe Lincoln said you can fool part of the people all of the time, but it is a long time since we have had occasion to see so many of our people fooled as from all accounts were fooled last Saturday night into giving up their $10 bills to donate to the Imperial Wizard and his Kleagles at the Klan meeting held near Norwood.

I understand they are looking for suckers in Ogdensburg and vicinity next Friday night, and somewhere else on Saturday night, and to those who have still a hold on their purse strings we would advise them to hold onto their cash until they find out how the suckers that signed-up at the Norwood meeting turn out.

This is not one of the things you can lose out by waiting for the Kleagle and his high-priced mouthpieces will be willing at any time later to take your cash.

Anyone that is 100 per cent. American can prove it better with a $10 bill than a K K K card or a uniform which they charged $5 extra for. The air of mystery which prevails at one of these meetings is one which appeals to some and they lose their sense of proportion. Look out, and when in Potsdam or vicinity buy your building supplies of W. F. ANDERSON whose red cedar shingles at 90cts a bunch are being talked about. Eleven bunches or a K K K Kard. Which will you spend your money for ?

W.F. Anderson's cedar shingle ad. *Republican Journal*, June 22, 1927. *New York State Historic Newspapers.*

The disappearance of the Black community from St. Lawrence County at the same time the KKK was attracting thousands of new members in the area is not a coincidence. All those letters written and crosses burned by "errant boys," as the newspapers often suggested, made that highly unlikely. The surviving local KKK charters, scare letters and national organization records paint a far different story of an era of rising hate, intolerance and intimidation in St. Lawrence County. By the late 1930s, the KKK's Hanmer was St. Lawrence County's presiding judge. A person happy to follow the moral dictates of the KKK, he used their influence to rise to local power and prominence.

The existing newspaper records show a troubling campaign of harassment of the Black population in Massena between 1918 and 1928. The Village of Massena hired Black construction workers to dig a canal at the intersection of Spruce Street and Liberty Avenue. Members of the Massena chapter of the KKK repeatedly marched up and down Spruce Street in protest.[105] Various Black citizens were ticketed repeatedly for minor violations such as speeding. When they were ticketed for possession of bootleg liquor, the fines of Black people were double those of white violators listed in the same newspaper.

Andrew McGee, a Black navy veteran who was about to marry and was purchasing a house in Massena in 1924, was charged with having an unlicensed revolver. He was fined fifty dollars. In 1925, he was charged with another unnamed misdemeanor. Judge Chase gave him the choice of jail time or leaving the area. Like so many others, he left the county. This type of sentence given only to a Black person or other visible minorities is clear evidence of local government support of efforts to remove Blacks and others from the county.

ALCOA corporation must be in some way involved in the loss of employment and the disappearance of the thirty-nine Black workers who were at the Massena plant in 1925. Many of these workers had been in Massena for more than five years. Not a single Black employee on the 1925 census purchased a house at Pine Grove, ALCOA's subsidized employee housing subdivision, or anywhere else in Massena or St. Lawrence County. From local records, it appears all Black families were gone from Massena by the 1927–28 school year. In April 1928, ALCOA advertised the Lincoln Hotel for sale. The formerly Blacks-only company hotel was now surplus property. The only way this could have happened was if ALCOA had stopped hiring and supporting its Black workers in the face of massive community opposition.

Some local residents claim it was the unionization of the plant by the white-only American Federation of Labor that led to the disappearance of the Black community. This is not plausible; the first union contract at the Massena plant was not finalized until 1934, but the majority of the Black population of Massena had already disappeared before 1928. The story of the vanished Black employees is one the community does not want to confront.

SUNY Potsdam student Gloria McDonald wrote a college paper on the KKK in Massena in 1975. At that time, she reported that the editor of the *Massena Observer*, Leonard Prince, claimed not to know what "KKK"

Black children playing on the Pine Grove Community Playground. *Aluminum Bulletin*, July 1920. *St. Lawrence County Historical Association Archives, Canton, New York.*

meant. This is not credible. In a tribute to Prince at the time of his death, editor Chuck Kelly wrote in the *Ogdensburg Journal*, "Leonard Prince was an institution in Massena, an unwavering Republican, a staunch Mason. He has been at the forefront as an active participant or as a news reporter of all major developments taking place in Massena since joining the *Observer* in 1928 as assistant editor."[106] Prince began his career as assistant editor of the *Observer* on September 13, 1928, just two weeks before the local Klan's notorious involvement in blood libel accusations of the local Jewish community.

Another local resident claimed Black people never made Massena their home because "they're either too smart to shovel the massive amount of snow, or they can't stand our cold Massena weather."[107] This is an unusual claim given that the 1930 census showed many of the former Black employees such as Lovick White were living in central New York, an area famous for its prodigious snowfalls. Leave Massena for Niagara Falls or Syracuse and you'll never shovel snow again? Not likely.

Between 1925 and 1930, the Black population of St. Lawrence County fell from 150 individuals to fewer than 50. In 1925, there were 37 Black men working for ALCOA (see appendix K); in 1930, there were 4. The majority of the Black residents remaining in 1930 were inmates of the St. Lawrence Psychiatric Hospital in Ogdensburg. These inmates came from throughout the state and mostly returned to their home communities upon release.

In comparison, in 1925, the Black population of Niagara Falls, New York, another ALCOA community, was double that of St. Lawrence County, at 300 individuals. It remained stable until World War II. By 1950, there were 3,000 Black people living in Niagara Falls. Would the Black population of St. Lawrence County have grown to 1,500 by 1950 if it had been allowed to remain, prosper and grow? We'll never know.

The removal of the Black population of St. Lawrence County in the late 1920s was no less a racial cleansing than others that were occurring throughout the United States in this same period. Massena lost not only families and workers but also musicians and athletes. These community losses were compounded by complicity in the coverup of the racial cleansing by the local newspapers and prominent citizens. Without knowledge of Black contributions paired with the intolerance, injustice and violence that undergirded that silence, we are denied a true understanding of the costs of racism in our county.

*This and following two pages*: Images of Black workers included in workers' collages. *Aluminum Bulletin*, September 1920. *St. Lawrence County Historical Association Archives, Canton, New York.*

# Timeline, Chapter 5

| | |
|---|---|
| 1901 September 14 | Theodore Roosevelt sworn in as president. |
| 1903 | ALCOA purchases aluminum smelting operation at Massena. |
| 1907 | ALCOA begins Pine Grove housing development to house workers. |
| 1909 | William Howard Taft sworn in as president. |
| 1913 | Woodrow Wilson sworn in as president. |
| 1915 August | State militia called in to end five-day strike at ALCOA. |
| 1915 | ALCOA begins recruiting Black workers for Massena operation, at times recruiting as many as two hundred a week. |
| 1916 | ALCOA turns Fiber Plant into temporary housing for Black workers. |
| 1917 | ALCOA uses Black strikebreakers in East St. Louis, Illinois. White mob kills over two hundred Black people. |
| 1917 October 3 | Bessie White murdered near new high school. |
| 1917 | Local Black workers are drafted into World War I. Curtis Snead serves honorably. |
| 1917 | Alexander Ellerby comes to Massena from Boston. |
| 1918 | ALCOA builds Lincoln Hotel to house Black workers. |
| 1918 | "Colored" recreation hall opened in Fiber Plant. |

| | |
|---|---|
| 1918 March | ALCOA begins publishing *Aluminum Bulletin*. |
| 1918 August | Mrs. L.E. Hopson becomes local reporter for the *Chicago Defender*. |
| 1918 August 9 | Article "Southern Tactics in Massena" appears in *Chicago Defender*. |
| 1918 August | The Reverend E.K. Harris begins holding "Colored" church services in ALCO gymnasium. |
| 1919 May | James Holmes and Junia Winbush married in Massena. |
| 1920 | Local papers first refer to the "Colored" section of Massena. |
| 1920 | Alexander Ellerby and his "colored" orchestra hold dances at Pine Grove Community center. He also manages the "Colored Giants," an ALCOA league Black baseball team. |
| 1921 | Warren Harding sworn in as president. |
| 1923 May | Judge Giles Chase sentences five Black women to leave town, continuing a practice in place since at least 1918 of banishing Black residents for the slightest of infractions. |
| 1923 August 2 | Calvin Coolidge sworn in as president. |
| 1923 August | Maggie and Lovick White, Black managers of the Lincoln Hotel, are arrested. Maggie dares to request a jury trial. Charges are dismissed for lack of evidence. |
| 1923 | Local press raise the specter of a local lynching in the case of John Washington Williams. Comes to naught. |

| | |
|---|---|
| 1925 | Army War College releases study "Use of Negro Manpower in War." Its pseudo-science is used to restrict Black access to higher education and reinforces popular racist myths. |
| 1926 | Hooded Ku Klux Klan (KKK) members demand St. Lawrence County DA William Ingram dismiss all Catholic workers in his office. He refuses. |
| 1926 July 3 | Rudolph Valentino Sims born at Massena, son of local Black worker. |
| 1926 September | DA Ingram wins primary challenge from Klan-endorsed A.J. Hanmer. |
| 1926 October | Maggie White again arrested. A jury trial follows; she is acquitted. She is arrested the next day for no visible means of support. |
| 1926 November 30 | Alexander Ellerby (former Negro League professional ballplayer) dies in Ogdensburg hospital of TB. |
| 1927 February | Maggie White given ten days to leave town. |
| 1927 | Massena chapter of KKK, Power City Klavern #212, chartered. |
| 1927 | Cross burned behind Kaufman's store on Main Street in Massena. |
| 1927 July 23 | Five thousand people attend KKK rally on Potsdam-Norwood Road. |
| 1927 | Local Klan marches repeatedly on Spruce Street in Massena in protest of Black workers hired to dig a canal. |
| 1927 December | Last recorded banishment of four Black women and one Black man by Judge Chase. |

| | |
|---|---|
| 1928 April | ALCOA advertises Lincoln Hotel for sale as surplus property. Rooming house for Black workers no longer needed. |
| 1928 September | Barbara Griffith lost in woods. Jewish community accused in only blood libel accusation in North America. |
| 1929 | Herbert Hoover sworn in as president. |
| 1930 | U.S. census shows four Black workers employed at ALCOA. |

# 1810 U.S. CENSUS

## BLACK RESIDENTS OF
## ST. LAWRENCE COUNTY

| Town/Resident | Number of Slaves Owned |
|---|:---:|
| **Madrid** | |
| Ephraim Hurlbut | 3 |
| Gouverneur Ogden | 5 |
| John Rice | 5 (crossed out) |
| **Lisbon** | |
| William Lyttle | 1 |
| Henry Yragg? | 1 |
| **Stockholm** | |
| Phineas Paulk | 1 |
| **Potsdam** | |
| William Carpenter | 2 |
| **Hopkinton** | |
| Phineas Paulk | 1 slave, 1 free non-white |
| **Oswegatchie** | |
| David Judson | 1 |
| Daniel N.P. Weil | 1 |

| Town/Resident | Number of Slaves Owned |
|---|---|
| Note Louis Hasbrouck enumerated Ulster Co. | 3 |
| **Cambray (Gouverneur)** | |
| Israel Porter | 1 |
| Ephraim C. Gates | 1 |
| **De Kalb** | |
| Daniel Smith | 1 |
| Isaac Stacy | 1 |
| **Massena** | |
| Naham Wilson | 5 |
| Nathan Olmstead | 8 |
| David White | 2 (crossed out) |
| **Canton** | |
| Henry Johnson | 1 |

# 1820 U.S. CENSUS

## BLACK RESIDENTS OF
## ST. LAWRENCE COUNTY

| Town | Less Than 14 | 14 to 26 | 26 to 45 | Over 45 |
|---|---|---|---|---|
| Pierrepont | | 1 male slave | | |
| De Kalb | | 1 male slave | | |
| | | 1 female slave | | |
| Russell | 1 male slave | | | |
| Potsdam | 1 free male | 1 free male | | |
| | 1 free female | | | |
| Oswegatchie | 2 female slaves | 2 female slaves | | |
| Oswegatchie | 1 free female | 2 free males | 3 free males | 1 free female |
| | | 2 free females | 2 free females | |

# 1825 New York State Census

## Black Residents of
## St. Lawrence County

| Town | Untaxed | Taxed | Taxed Highest Rate |
|------|---------|-------|--------------------|
| Oswegatchie | 13 | 5 | 2 |
| Potsdam | 1 | | |
| Madrid | 3 | | |
| Canton | 1 | | |
| Stockholm | | 3 | |
| Fowler | 8 | | |
| Hopkinton | | | 1 |
| Gouverneur | 1 | | |
| Pierrepont | 1 | | |
| Massena | 11 | 1 | |
| Morristown | 5 | | |
| De Kalb | 2 | | |
| De Peyster | 1 | | |
| Russell | 1 | | |
| Lisbon | 2 | | |

Only Black men who had over $250 in property (taxed highest rate) could vote for governor.

# 1830 U.S. CENSUS

## BLACK RESIDENTS OF
## ST. LAWRENCE COUNTY

| Town | Black Head of Household | Number of People in House |
|---|---|---|
| Oswegatchie | James Nash | 6 |
| | Josiah Morris | 11 |
| | John Thompson | 4 |
| | Joseph Sharp | 5 |
| | John Shaver | 2 |
| Massena | Richard Boston | 11 |
| Potsdam | William Dixon | 1 |
| | White Head of Household with Black Members | Number of Black Members of Household |
| Oswegatchie | Rawling Webster | 1 male under 10 |
| | Eri Lusher | 1 male 10 to 24 |
| | Joseph W. Smith | 1 male 10 to 24 |
| | Elijah Allen | 1 male 10 to 24<br>1 female 10 to 24 |
| | Jesse Shaver | 1 male 36 to 55 |
| | Jacob Van Heuvel | 1 female 10 to 24 |

| Town | White Head of Household with Black Members | Number of Black Members of Household |
|---|---|---|
| De Kalb | Charles Borland | 1 female 24 to 36 |
| Canton | Jonathan Langden | 1 male under 10 |
| | Dr. Olin | 1 male under 10 |
| Massena | John Perkins | 1 female 24 to 36 |
| | Joseph Residue or Willard Seaten | 1 female 24 to 36 |
| Madrid | William Ogden | 1 female 55 to 100 |
| | Jason Fenton | 1 female 55 to 100 |
| Potsdam | Samuel Partidge | 1 female 10 to 24 |
| | Isaac Elly | 1 female under 10 |
| | Wm. H. Leray | 1 male 10 to 24 |

# 1835 NEW YORK STATE CENSUS

## BLACK RESIDENTS OF
## ST. LAWRENCE COUNTY

| Town | Not Taxed | Taxed | Voters |
|---|---|---|---|
| De Kalb | 1 | | |
| Lisbon | 1 | | |
| Massena | 5 | 1 | |
| Oswegatchie | 44 | 1 | |
| Potsdam | 4 | | |
| Stockholm | 1 | | |

In order to vote, Black men had to own $250 in property; hence, "taxed" meant able to vote if a man.

# 1845 NEW YORK STATE CENSUS

## BLACK RESIDENTS OF
## ST. LAWRENCE COUNTY

| Town | Not Taxed | Taxed | Voters |
|------|-----------|-------|--------|
| Brasher | 3 | | |
| Canton | 1 | | |
| De Kalb | 1 | | |
| De Peyster | 1 | | |
| Fowler | 1 | | |
| Gouverneur | 5 | | |
| Hammond | 2 | | |
| Louisville | 1 | | |
| Lisbon | 2 | | |
| Massena | 3 | 2 | 1 |
| Oswegatchie | 14 | | |
| Rossie | 1 | | |

In order to vote, Black men had to own $250 in property; hence, "taxed" meant able to vote if a man.

# 1855 NEW YORK STATE CENSUS

## Black Residents of
## St. Lawrence County

| Town | Males | Females | Not Taxed | Taxed | Voters |
|------|-------|---------|-----------|-------|--------|
| Brasher | | 1 | 1 | | |
| Colton | 1 | | 1 | | |
| De Kalb | | 1 | 1 | | |
| Gouverneur | 4 | 3 | 7 | | |
| Lisbon | 19 | 18 | 32 | 5 | |
| Louisville | 7 | 5 | 12 | | |
| Massena | 7 | 1 | 5 | 3 | |
| Norfolk | 2 | 7 | 1 | 8 | |
| Oswegatchie | 10 | 15 | 25 | | |
| Potsdam | | 1 | 1 | | |

In order to vote, Black men had to own $250 in property; hence, "taxed" meant able to vote if a man.

# 1865 NEW YORK STATE CENSUS

## BLACK RESIDENTS OF
## ST. LAWRENCE COUNTY

| Town | Not Taxed |
|------|-----------|
| Gouverneur | 1 |
| Louisville | 15 |
| Madrid | 5 |
| Massena | 6 |
| Oswegatchie | 5 |
| Parishville | 4 |

Black residents who were taxed were not enumerated in 1865.

# 1875 NEW YORK STATE CENSUS

## Black Residents of
## St. Lawrence County

| Town | Males | Females |
|------|-------|---------|
| Canton | 1 | |
| De Peyster | 3 | 4 |
| Gouverneur | 1 | 1 |
| Hammond | 1 | 1 |
| Lawrence | | 1 |
| Louisville | 10 | 5 |
| Madrid | 1 | 6 |
| Massena | 6 | 7 |
| Oswegatchie | 3 | 2 |
| Ogdensburg (Wards 1, 3, 4) | 18 | 17 |
| Parishville | 2 | 4 |
| Potsdam | 4 | 8 |
| Waddington | 6 | 4 |
| **Total** | **56** | **60** |

# 1920 U.S. CENSUS

## BLACK WORKERS AT MASSENA

| Name | Age | Citizenship | Occupation |
|---|---|---|---|
| Alexander, Alec | 43 | NC | Pot man |
| Barrows, Mauel | 32 | Cape Verde | Pot man |
| Belamy, Manuel | 20 | West Indies | Pot man |
| Brown, Henry | 23 | PR | Pot man |
| Brown, James | 29 | MD | Pot man |
| Byrd, Bergon | 21 | GA | Pot man |
| Ceasar, Edward | 59 | NY | Carbon Plant |
| Colson, Charles | 50 | FL | Pot man |
| Cook, George | 24 | NY | None |
| Cooper, George | 24 | NY | Bull gang |
| Cunningham, John | 35 | NY | Pot man |
| Daniels, Clifford | 25 | GA | Pot man |
| Dibble, LeRoy | 17 | VA | Grocery |
| Ennis, Armando | 25 | Portugal | Pot man |
| Everslay, Samuel | 36 | British Guyana | Pot man |
| Frank, Easley | 28 | GA | Laborer Alum. Co. |

| Name | Age | Citizenship | Occupation |
|------|-----|-------------|------------|
| Grass, Ernest | 22 | VA | Pot man |
| Hanley, Fred | 25 | VA | Pot man |
| Harris, Eli | 48 | AL | Pot man |
| Henry, Fred | 33 | KY | Pot man |
| Henry, William | 32 | NY | Bull gang |
| Hines, Joseph | 36 | OH | Pot man |
| Hopson, Frank | 34 | MN | Pot man |
| Jackson, Ernest | 25 | NY | Pot man |
| Jeffrey, Charles | 19 | NY | Bull gang |
| Jones, William | 23 | NY | Pot man |
| Lassie, Victor | 27 | Cape Verde | Pressroom |
| Leda, Edward | 31 | Cuba | Pot man |
| LeRue, Victor | 21 | PR | Pot man |
| Levery, Arthur | 21 | AL | Pot man |
| Mackealbrt, J. | 21 | AL | Pot man |
| Manuel, Bronco | 25 | Portugal | Pot man |
| Markey, Patrick | 25 | IR | Carbon Plant |
| Medford, William | 40 | Cuba | Pot man |
| Mehres, Eugene | 35 | Cuba | Pot man |
| Melieb, Anthony | 23 | VA | Pot man |
| Montiero, Louis | 31 | Portugal | Pot man |
| Neal, William | 31 | GA | Pot man |
| Pereva, Tony | 28 | Portugal | Pot man |
| Perez, Secundio | 27 | Panama | Pot man |
| Perry, John M. | 41 | Cape Verde | Laborer Alum. Co. |
| Perry, Joseph | 22 | MA | Pot man |
| Perry, Thomas | 25 | Brazil | Pot man |
| Philbert, Landon | 43 | LA | Pressroom |

| Name | Age | Citizenship | Occupation |
|------|-----|-------------|------------|
| Ross, William | 26 | AK | Pot room |
| Rush, Silas | 42 | NY | Pot room |
| See, William | 33 | NY | Wire mill |
| Soares, Joseph | 26 | Portugal | Pot man |
| Swift, Phillip | 30 | PR | Pot man |

# 1925 NEW YORK STATE CENSUS

## BLACK WORKERS AT ALCOA

| Name | Age | Citizenship | Occupation |
|------|-----|-------------|------------|
| Manuel Barrows | 35 | US | Foundry Laborer |
| Christopher Battershell | 44 | Barbados | Pot Man |
| Herkia Brown | 38 | US | Laborer Plant |
| Floyd Cheatham | 32 | US | Foundry Laborer |
| Bruce Clark | 45 | US | Foundry Laborer |
| Herbert G. Clark | 33 | British West Indies | Foundry Laborer |
| Charles L. Colson | 54 | US | Fishman |
| George W. Cooper | 42 | US | Foundry Laborer |
| Lindsay Cross | 30 | Canadian | Foundry Laborer |
| George Dennis | 46 | US | Foundry Laborer |
| Lawrence Dennis | 18 | US | Foundry Laborer |
| Alex R. Ellerby | 58 | US | Foundry Laborer |
| Clarence Finney | 24 | US | Foundry Laborer |
| Eliza H. Harris | 48 | US | Foundry Laborer |
| Joseph Hayes | 38 | US | Foundry Laborer |

| Name | Age | Citizenship | Occupation |
|------|-----|-------------|------------|
| J.W. Holmes | 38 | US | Housekeeper |
| Henry C. Howard | 32 | US | Foundry Laborer |
| Jerry Jenkins | 31 | US | Foundry Laborer |
| Amos Johnson | 26 | US | Foundry Laborer |
| Henry Johnson | 35 | US | Foundry Laborer |
| William Johnson | 36 | US | Foundry Laborer |
| Philbert Landon | 40 | US | Laborer Carbon Plant |
| Archie Louden | 40 | US | Foundry Laborer |
| Solomon Lowe | 22 | US | Laborer Carbon Plant |
| Walter McClegrey | 34 | US | Foundry Laborer |
| Andrew McGee | 36 | US | Foundry Laborer |
| Antumino Percez | 30 | Panama | Pot Man |
| Joseph Perry | 27 | US | Foundry Laborer |
| Joseph Reynolds | 21 | US | Foundry Laborer |
| James M. Sims | 43 | US | Foundry Laborer |
| Milton E. Sims | 19 | US | Foundry Laborer |
| George W. Taylor | 42 | US | Foundry Laborer |
| Robert Tyren | 38 | US | Laborer Plant |
| Manuel Vozquer | 44 | US | Foundry Laborer |
| Richard Walker | 39 | US | Foundry Laborer |
| William Ward | 42 | US | Laborer ALCO |
| John Wardell | 27 | US | Foundry Laborer |
| Lovick White | 27 | US | Foundry Laborer |
| Robert Williams | 32 | US | Foundry Laborer |

# NOTES

## Chapter 1

1. *Panis* is a unique French-Canadian term for Indigenous American slaves.
2. Archives nationales du Québec, Centre de Québec, Ordonnances des intendants, E1, S1, P509, Jacques Raudot, ordinance relative to slavery in Canada, April 13, 1709.
3. Boyesen, "French and Indian Settlement at Ogdensburg," 8–9.
4. The Oswegatchie, as they were called, were Onondaga, Oneida, Cayuga, Abenaki, Mississagua and other scattered nations all brought together by Abbé Piquet under the banner of his Christian mission.
5. Boyesen, "French Personnel at la Présentation," 15.
6. Hough, *History of St. Lawrence and Franklin Counties*, 63–65.
7. Ibid.

## Chapter 2

8. Berlin, *Many Thousands Gone*.
9. Laws of New York State, vol. 3, ch. 60.
10. *St. Lawrence Plaindealer*, May 17, 1938.
11. Hough, *History of St. Lawrence and Franklin Counties*, 594.

12. Joseph Hasbrouck to Louis Hasbrouck, January 7, 1812, Clements Library, University of Michigan, Ann Arbor.

13. Eliza Graham to Catherine Hasbrouck, August 1, 1805, Clements Library, University of Michigan, Ann Arbor.

14. Sarah Lasher to Catherine Hasbrouck, July 15, 1809, Clements Library, University of Michigan, Ann Arbor.

15. Eliza Graham to Catherine Hasbrouck, August 1, 1805, Clements Library, University of Michigan, Ann Arbor.

16. Sarah Lasher to Catherine Hasbrouck, October 6, 1812, Clements Library, University of Michigan, Ann Arbor.

17. Catherine Hasbrouck to Louis Hasbrouck, November 19, 1812, Clements Library, University of Michigan, Ann Arbor.

18. Ulster County Probate Court, Wills Liber, p. 274, estate of Andries Roosa 1802.

19. Hasbrouck Family Papers Box 5, letter, June 13, 1817, L. Hasbrouck to C. Hasbrouck. Op. cit.

20. Joseph Hasbrouck to Louis Hasbrouck, July 18, 1815.

21. Mr. Gregory to Isaac Cooper, March 16, 1813, Judge William Cooper Papers, Hartwick College, Oneonta, NY.

22. John Fine to Isaac Cooper, November 14, 1815, Judge William Cooper Papers, Hartwick College, Oneonta, NY. A transcription of this letter and others can be found at "The Judge William Cooper Papers: The De Kalb Correspondence," Historian's Office, Town of De Kalb, NY, www.dekalbnyhistorian.org/CooperLetters/IsaacCooper/1815Nov14JFine.pdf.

23. Fine to Cooper, November 14, 1815.

24. Charlotte Ogden diary, St. Lawrence County Historical Association Archives, Canton, NY.

25. "A Pillar of Zion," obituary of Christopher Rush, *Christian Recorder*, August 7, 1873, www.accessible.com.dbgateway.nysed.gov/accessible/print.

26. Dorine's grandfather was known as Cato and was the slave of the Gouverneur Ogden family.

27. Pringle, *Lunenburgh or the Old Eastern District*, 323–24.

28. St. Lawrence County Clerk, Mortgages Liber 2: 311, St. Lawrence County Clerk's Office, Canton, NY.

29. St. Lawrence County Clerk, New York, Deeds Liber 5: 630.

## Chapter 3

30. St. Lawrence Academy Attendance Records, Special Collections, Potsdam Public Museum, Potsdam, NY.

31. Burgess and Ward, *Free Baptist Cyclopædia*; "Anti-Slavery Society," Freewill Baptist Records, MC091. This encyclopedia can also be found online at archive.org/details/freebaptistscycl00burg/page/18/mode/2up.

32. Obituary of George McEwen, *Ogdensburg Journal*, November 7, 1877, nyshistoricnewspapers.org/lccn/sn85054113/1877-11-07/ed-1/seq-3.

33. Lewis, *Life, Labors and Travels of Elder Charles W. Bowles*, 23–24.

34. Ibid., 30.

35. St. Lawrence County Clerk, Deeds Liber 22: 278, St. Lawrence County Clerk's Office, Canton, NY.

36. Lewis, *Life, Labors and Travels of Elder Charles W. Bowles*, 207.

37. Ibid., 147–48.

38. St. Lawrence County Clerk, Deeds Liber 39B: 165.

39. Ursula Johnson, U.S. Census, City of Auburn, 1850, 1860, 1870. All three censuses list Ursula's birthdate as 1823.

40. New York State Census, Town of LeRay, Jefferson County, 4, Danby Fry, 1835, Jefferson County Clerk's Office, Watertown, NY.

41. U.S. Census of the Bureau, Town of Gouverneur, Danby Fry, 1850, 1860, HeritageQuest Online.

42. U.S. Census of the Bureau, Town of Gouverneur, household #437, 1850.

43. I have retained the use of the word "colored" to describe Civil War military units of African Americans, since official names included that term.

44. Lavinia Fry, Widows Pension File #362810, Civil War Widows' Pension Files, U.S. National Archives and Records Administration, Washington, D.C. Copy in possession of author.

45. Rensselaer County Surrogate Court, Probate File #660, Roll 184 #62, Troy, NY.

## Chapter 4

46. Jim Holland, interview by author, August 2002. Talking about Charles Clark, Holland stated, "They brought back six slaves you know."

47. The hamlet of De Kalb is known locally as Old De Kalb.

48. Interview with June Holland Gabriels, July 2008.

49. Canton Town Clerk, death certificate of Charles Clark, Canton, NY.

50. Both the 1870 and 1880 censuses give her maiden name as Hayden. Her obituary gives it as Hazen.

51. Canton Town Clerk, death certificate of Nancy Tompkins.

52. Those arrested were Harold Thoms, Charles Broeffle, William Walsh, Adrian Scott, Leslie McMonagle, Clarence Tipson, Alton Purvee, James Heffernan, Hymie Wheeler, Clarence Denesha, Clarence Grotto, William Myers and Howard Hill.

53. "Rev. George S. Brown: Methodist Minister, Missionary and Master Stone Mason," *North Country Lantern* (newsletter of North Country Underground Railroad Historical Association) (Summer/Fall 2008), northcountryundergroundrailroad.com/newsletters/Newsletter-Summer-Fall-2008.pdf.

54. U.S. Census Bureau, Town of Potsdam, 1860, HeritageQuest Online.

55. "G.B. Swan Colored," *The Liberator*, March 20, 1863, 47.

56. The Bucks Bridge Antislavery Society was formed in 1834, the same year in which anti-Black riots broke out in New York City.

57. *Daily Journal* (Ogdensburg), July 3, 1868.

58. *Albany Evening Journal*, August 31, 1872.

59. *Daily Journal* (Ogdensburg, NY), October 14, 1880, 3.

60. St. Lawrence County Surrogate's Court, file 6020.

61. "DeKalb," *Gouverneur [NY] Free Press*, August 19, 1885.

62. U.S. Census Bureau, Town of De Kalb, 1860, Household #446.

63. *Daily Journal* (Ogdensburg, NY), January 22, 1867. This article largely reiterated "Excitement at De Kalb" in the previous day's paper.

64. "Criminal Cases," *St. Lawrence Republican*, July 2, 1867.

65. St. Lawrence County Court of Special Sessions, Vol. 3:320.

66. "DeKalb," *Gouverneur [NY] Free Press*, August 26, 1885.

67. "The Green Murder Trial," *Commercial Advertiser* (Canton, NY), May 20, 1886.

68. Ibid.

69. Ibid.

70. "Sensation of 1867 Recalled by De Kalb Man," *Norwood [NY] News*, March 18, 1914.

71. All Edward Green's children were listed as illiterate on the censuses of 1870 and 1880. New York State law allowed school commissioners to educate Black children but did not require that they do so.

## Chapter 5

72. *New York Times*, October 8, 1924

73. *New York Times*, August 2, 1915.

74. Henry Clay Frick, an industrialist with links to both Andrew Mellon and Andrew Carnegie, was well known as an anti-union business leader.

75. Stoller, *Goliath.*

76. Ibid.

77. *Madrid Herald*, May 11, 1916.

78. *Republican Journal*, October 5, 1917.

79. Friedman, *Incident at Massena.*

80. "Race men" was a term used in the Black press of the time for Black men.

81. *Chicago Defender*, August 10, 1918

82. Ibid.

83. *Aluminum Bulletin*, August 1918.

84. *Aluminum Bulletin*, February 1919.

85. *Aluminum Bulletin*, August 1919.

86. One example of several Black couples' marriages confirmed through license applications.

87. *Massena Observer*, October 11, 1923.

88. *Watertown Daily Times*, February 4, 1922.

89. *Aluminum Bulletin*, June 1920.

90. *The Massena Observer*, December 9, 1926.

91. *New York Times*. October 7, 1924.

92. *Republican Journal* (Ogdensburg, NY), December 7, 1922.

93. *Republican Journal*, September 17, 1928.

94. *Potsdam Herald-Recorder*, December 8, 1922.

95. *Republican Journal*, January 17, 1928.

96. *Republican Journal*, December 5, 1924

97. *Ogdensburg Journal*, May 14, 1925.

98. *Gouverneur Free Press*, September 15, 1926.

99. *Courier Freeman*, November 17, 1926.

100. *Northern Tribune* (Gouverneur, NY), September 15, 1926.

101. Hanmer would eventually succeed Ingram as DA when Ingram became a county judge. When Ingram died in office, Hanmer succeeded him again as county judge.

102. *Chicago Defender*, December 15, 1928.

103. *Commercial Advertiser*, January 20, 1925.

104. *Massena Observer*, May 24, 1923.

105. Mrs. Robert Dupree [Gloria McDonald Dupree] to Richard White, February 5, 1978; White to author, July 3, 2019. Both letters are in the possession of the author.

106. *Ogdensburg Journal*, September 17, 1975.

107. Dupree to White, February 5, 1978; White to author, July 3, 2019. Both letters are in the possession of the author.

# SELECTED BIBLIOGRAPHY

## *Chapter 1*

Bonaparte, Darren. *An Early History of Akwesasne: The Works of Franklin B. Hough*. June 3, 2020.

—. "The Seven Nations of Canada and the Treaty of 1796." Presented at the St. Regis Mohawk Tribe's monthly meeting of May 11, 2019.

Boyesen, Persis Yates. "The French and Indian Settlement at Ogdensburg." *St. Lawrence County Historical Association Quarterly* 35, no. 1 (January 1990): 4–10.

—. "French Personnel at la Présentation." *St. Lawrence County Historical Association Quarterly* 35, no. 1 (January 1990): 11–15.

Cooper, Afua. *The Hanging of Angélique: The Untold Story of Canadian Slavery and the Burning of Old Montréal*. Toronto: HarperCollins Publisher, 2006.

Hough, Franklin B. *A History of St. Lawrence and Franklin Counties, New York: From the Earliest Period to the Present Time*. Albany, NY: Little and Company, 1853.

Trudel, Marcel. *Dictionnaire des esclaves et de leurs propriétaires au Canada français*. 2nd edition. Montréal: Hurtubise, 1994.

—. *L'esclavage au Canada français: histoire et conditions de l'esclavage*. Québec City: Presses de l'Université Laval, 1960.

# Chapter 2

Beers, S.N., and D.G. Beers. *New Topographical Atlas of St. Lawrence County New York*. Philadelphia: Stone and Stewart Publishers, 1865.

Berlin, Ira. *Many Thousands Gone: The First Two Centuries of Slavery in North America*. Cambridge, MA: Harvard University Press, 1988.

Censuses of the State of New York. St. Lawrence County, 1814, 1825, 1855. New York State Library, Digital Collections, Historical Documents, NYS Census. www.nysl.nysed.gov/scandocs/nyscensus.htm.

*Christian Recorder* (Philadelphia), August 7, 1873. "A Pillar of Zion," obituary of Christopher Rush. www.accessible.com.dbgateway.nysed.gov/accessible/print.

Fine, John. Letter to Isaac Cooper, November 1815. Judge William Cooper Papers. Paul F. Cooper Jr. Archives. Hartwick College, Oneonta, NY.

Gregory, Mr. Letter to Isaac Cooper, March 16, 1813. Judge William Cooper Papers. Paul F. Cooper Jr. Archives. Hartwick College, Oneonta, NY.

Hasbrouck Papers. Box 3, 4, 5 Clements Library, University of Michigan, Ann Arbor, MI.

———. Two Bills of Sale for Slaves. Ogdensburg Public Library Archives, Ogdensburg, NY.

Hough, Franklin. *A History of St. Lawrence and Franklin Counties*. Albany, NY: Little and Company, 1853.

New York. Laws of New York State, 1799, Chapter 62; 1801, Chapter 188; 1802, Chapter 52; 1804, Chapter 60; 1817. St. Lawrence County Law Library, Canton, NY.

Ogden, Charlotte. Ogden Family Diary: Waddington Box 2. St. Lawrence County Historical Association Archives, Canton, NY.

Pringle, J.F. *Lunenburgh or the Old Eastern District: Its Settlement and Early Progress*. Cornwall, ON: Standard Printing House, 1890.

St. Lawrence County Clerk. Deeds Liber 5 page 630. St. Lawrence County Clerk's Office, Canton, NY.

———. Mortgages Liber 2 page 311. St. Lawrence County Clerk's Office, Canton, NY.

*St. Lawrence Plaindealer*. "Attestation of David Ford." May 17, 1938. Owen D. Young Library, St. Lawrence University, Canton, NY.

———. May 7, 1938. Owen D. Young Library, St. Lawrence University, Canton, NY.

Taylor, Alan. *William Cooper's Town: Power and Persuasion on the Frontier of the Early American Republic*. New York: Vintage Books, 1995.

Ulster County Surrogate Court. Wills Liber C: 274 Estate of Andries Roosa, 1802. Kingston, NY.

U.S. Census Bureau. St. Lawrence County, NY, 1800, 1810, 1820, 1830, 1840, 1850.

## *Chapter 3*

Burgess, G.A., and J.T. Ward. *Free Baptist Cyclopædia: Historical and Biographical.* N.p.: Free Baptist Cyclopædia Co., 1889.

The Free-Will Baptist Church. *The Annual Report of the Free-Will Baptist Anti-Slavery Society.* Dover, NH: William Burr Printer, 1848.

Freewill Baptist Records, MC091. Edmund S. Muskie Archives and Special Collections Library, Bates College, Lewiston, ME.

The Free-Will Baptist Register, 1839–64. Yearly Meeting Reports. Dover, NH.

Free-Will Baptist Trustees. Minutes of the Eighth General Conference of the Free-Will Baptist Connection, 1836. Dover, NH.

French's Auburn City Directory, 1870, 1871, 1872. Seymour Library, Auburn, NY.

Fry, Lavinia, Widows Pension File #362810. The Civil War Widows' Pension Files. The U.S. National Archives and Records Administration, Washington, D.C.

Hough, Franklin. *A History of St. Lawrence and Franklin Counties.* Albany, NY: Little and Company, 1853.

Lewis, John W. *The Life, Labors and Travels of Elder Charles W. Bowles of the Freewill Baptist Denomination.* Watertown, NY: Ingalls and Stowell's Steam Press, 1852. docsouth.unc.edu/neh/lewisjw/lewisjw.html.

McKivigan, John R. *The War Against Proslavery Religion: Abolitionism and the Northern Churches.* Ithaca, NY: Cornell University Press, 1984.

New York County (Manhattan) Surrogate Court. Probate Department. 1909 Roll 717 #16520, Death Certificate for Robert Fry. New York.

New York State Adjutant General's Office Civil War Muster Roll Abstracts of New York State Volunteers, United States Sharpshooters, and United States Colored Troops, Series 13775-83: Box 720: Roll 376, New York State Archives, Albany, NY.

New York State Census. Auburn Ward 3, 1855. Ancestry: New York State Records. www.archives.nysed.gov/research/how-to-video-ancestry.

———. Town of LeRay, 4, 1835. Jefferson County Clerk's Office, Watertown, NY.

O'Reilly, Henry. "First Organization of Colored Troops in the State of New York, to Aid in Suppressing the Slaveholders' Rebellion: Statements Concerning the Origin, Difficulties and Success of the Movement, Including Official Documents, Military Testimonials, Proceedings of the 'Union League Club,' Etc." New York: Baker & Godwin, Printers, 1864. Internet Archive. archive.org/stream/firstorganizationewy/firstorganizationewy_djvu.txt.

Rensselaer County Surrogate Court. Probate File #660, Roll 184, #62, Troy, NY.

"St. Lawrence Anti-Slavery Convention." *Friend of Man* (Utica, NY), October 4, 1837. Cornell University Collection. fom.library.cornell.edu/?a=d&d=TFOM18371004.2.1&srpos=1&e=-------en-20--1--txt-txIN-october+4+1837------.

St. Lawrence County Clerk. Deeds Liber 51C: 41; Deed Liber 76B: 255; Deed Liber 77C: 499; Deed Liber 86B: 205; Deed Liber 170C: 1863. St. Lawrence County Clerk's Office, Canton, NY.

St. Lawrence County Surrogate Court. Probate File # 3234, Canton, NY.

U.S. Census of the Bureau. HeritageQuest Online, New York State Library, Databases and E-Journals. www.nysl.nysed.gov/gate/esubject.htm.

———. City of Auburn (Cayuga County), 1850, 1860, 1870, 1880.

———. Town of Champion (Jefferson County), 1800, 1810, 1820.

———. Town of Gouverneur (St. Lawrence County), 1840, 1850, 1860, 1870, 1880, 1900.

———. Town of Philadelphia (Jefferson County), 1830.

Wiley, Susan Caulkins. *The First Ten Decades of the Town of Champion.* N.p., n.d. Genealogy Department, Rosewell P. Flower Memorial Library, Watertown, NY.

## *Chapter 4*

*Advance News* (Ogdensburg, NY). "Snatching of Bodies Recalled." September 5, 1948.

*Albany [NY] Evening Journal*, August 31, 1872.

*Canton [NY] Plaindealer.* "Twenty Years Ago." July 10, 1914. Ogdensburg Public Library Archives. Newspaper Collection. Ogdensburg, NY. (Most articles are also available online from Northern New York Library Network, NYS Historic Newspapers, nyshistoricnewspapers.org.)

*Commercial Advertiser* (Canton, NY), February 12, 1924. Ogdensburg Public Library Archives. Newspaper Collection. Ogdensburg, NY. (Most articles are also available online from Northern New York Library Network, NYS Historic Newspapers, nyshistoricnewspapers.org.)

———. "At the Bar." July 26, 1932.

———. "Bassett Woods Like Days of Old." September 19, 1933.

———. "Canton Red Cross Branch Quota." May 28, 1918.

———. "Card of Thanks." July 7, 1914.

———. "County Ward Picked Up Change on Side, in Trouble." February 13, 1940.

———. "Death by Train." November 1, 1927.

———. "Did Jake Tompkins or Didn't Jake Tompkins and Circus Bear." July 6, 1937.

———. "Fined $10 for Body Snatching." February 15, 1916.

———. "Fire Takes Two Dwellings on Dies Street." February 1, 1927.

———. "The Green Murder Trial." May 20, 1886.

———. "Jake Tompkins Does a Little Fishing." January 19, 1932.

———. "Joe Infantine Gets Big Brown Trout on Jordan River." June 21, 1932.

———. "Little Stories of Old Morley." November 2, 1937.

———. "Looking Through a Main Street Window." January 30, 1945.

———. "Lots of Fishermen but Few Fish as Trout Season Opens." April 4, 1939.

———. "Notice." April 29, 1930.

———. "Tells the Story of Walker Tompkins." August 24, 1937.

———. "Walter Leonard Refreshes Recollections of Old Timer." January 13, 1931.

*Courier and Freeman* (Potsdam, NY), January 16, 1879; September 7, 1904. Ogdensburg Public Library Archives. Newspaper Collection. Ogdensburg, NY. (Most articles are also available online from Northern New York Library Network, NYS Historic Newspapers, nyshistoricnewspapers.org.)

———. "Canton." July 1, 1914

———. "Tragedy in Lisbon." August 12, 1885.

*Daily Journal* (Ogdensburg, NY), January 22, 1867; July 3, 1868; October 14, 1880. Ogdensburg Public Library Archives. Newspaper Collection. Ogdensburg, NY. (Most articles are also available online from Northern New York Library Network, NYS Historic Newspapers, nyshistoricnewspapers.org.)

———. "The Case of Dr. Miller," January 28, 1867.

———. "Excitement at De Kalb," January 21, 1867.

*Gouverneur [NY] Free Press*, March 8, 1916. Ogdensburg Public Library Archives. Newspaper Collection. Ogdensburg, NY. (Most articles are also available online from Northern New York Library Network, NYS Historic Newspapers, nyshistoricnewspapers.org.)

———. "DeKalb." August 19, 1885.

———. "DeKalb." August 26, 1885.

———. "Robbed the Rich to Aid the Poor." March 5, 1924.

*Hammond [NY] Advertiser*, May 20, 1886; October 31, 1889. Ogdensburg Public Library Archives. Newspaper Collection. Ogdensburg, NY. (Most articles are also available online from Northern New York Library Network, NYS Historic Newspapers, nyshistoricnewspapers.org.)

*The Liberator.* "G.B. Swan Colored." March 20, 1863.

*Massena [NY] Observer*, March 12, 1916; September 8, 1904. Ogdensburg Public Library Archives. Newspaper Collection. Ogdensburg, NY. (Most articles are also available online from Northern New York Library Network, NYS Historic Newspapers, nyshistoricnewspapers.org.)

Miller, Richard F. *Flames Like Hades.* Auburn, NY: Finger Lakes Press, 2017.

*New York Times.* "Daniel Magone Dead." September 5, 1904.

———. "New Collector Named." August 11, 1886.

———. "Uniting North and South." February 23, 1887.

*North Country Lantern.* "Rev. George S. Brown: Methodist Minister, Missionary and Master Stone Mason." Summer/Fall 2008. northcountryundergroundrailroad.com/newsletters/Newsletter-Summer-Fall-2008.pdf.

*Norwood [NY] News*, June 19, 1890. Ogdensburg Public Library Archives. Newspaper Collection. Ogdensburg, NY. (Most articles are also available online from Northern New York Library Network, NYS Historic Newspapers, nyshistoricnewspapers.org.)

———. "Death Notice of Martha Raymond." August 25, 1885.

———. "Death of John Raymond." February 10, 1880.

———. "Sensation of 1867 Recalled by De Kalb Man." March 18, 1914.

*Ogdensburg [NY] Advance and St. Lawrence Weekly Democrat*, April 2, 1885; March 2, 1916. Ogdensburg Public Library Archives. Newspaper Collection. Ogdensburg, NY. (Most articles are also available online from Northern New York Library Network, NYS Historic Newspapers, nyshistoricnewspapers.org.)

———. "Barber Fined $10 for Theft." February 11, 1940.

————. "The Green Murder." May 13, 1886.

————. "Morley." July 9, 1914.

————. "Poker Game Invaded by the Police." January 23, 1940.

————. "Retells the Story of Rise of Potter Rice." February 7, 1924.

*Ogdensburg [NY] Journal*, January 22, 1867; July 2, 1867; July 18, 1874; November 3, 1875; May 11, 1876; August 29, 1878; December 14, 1878. Ogdensburg Public Library Archives. Newspaper Collection. Ogdensburg, NY. (Most articles are also available online from Northern New York Library Network, NYS Historic Newspapers, nyshistoricnewspapers.org.)

————. "The Arrest of W.B. Green." September 2, 1885.

————. "Chapel of My Dreams." February 1, 1936.

————. "A Colorful Character." March 11, 1936.

————. "Court Proceedings." January 3, 1879.

————. "The Green Murder Trial." May 12, 1886.

————. "The Killing of Green." August 11, 1885.

————. "The People Vs. Edward H. Green." December 21, 1868.

————. "A Terrible Tragedy in Lisbon," "The Testimony in the Case and the Verdict." August 10, 1885.

*Potsdam [NY] Herald-Recorder.* Ogdensburg Public Library Archives. Newspaper Collection. Ogdensburg, NY. (Most articles are also available online from Northern New York Library Network, NYS Historic Newspapers, nyshistoricnewspapers.org.)

————. "Fifty One Lives Lost." July 5, 1918.

St. Lawrence County Court of Special Sessions. Vol. 3:320 (May 12, 1885), Judgment Against Edward Green. Canton, NY.

St. Lawrence County Sessions Court. Minutes, Vol. 2:421 (January 1, 1879), Judgment Against Edward Green, Canton, NY.

St. Lawrence County Surrogate's Court. File 6249, Petition for Administration of the Goods Chattels and Credits of Edward Green. File 620, Estate Inventory of George B. Swan, Canton, NY.

*St. Lawrence Herald* (Potsdam, NY). "The Green Murder Trial." May 14, 1886.

*St. Lawrence Plaindealer* (Canton, NY). "Homicide." August 17, 1885.

*St. Lawrence Republican* (Ogdensburg, NY). Ogdensburg Public Library Archives. Newspaper Collection. Ogdensburg, NY. (Most articles are also available online from Northern New York Library Network, NYS Historic Newspapers, nyshistoricnewspapers.org.)

————. "Chain Store Seeks Lease from Healey." February 21, 1930.

———. "Criminal Cases." July 2, 1867.

———. "The De Kalb Grave Robbing Case." January 22, 1867.

———. "Walker Tompkins of Canton, Loses Life—Aged Man Walking Tracks." November 1, 1927.

U.S. Census Bureau. HeritageQuest Online, New York State Library, Databases and E-Journals. www.nysl.nysed.gov/gate/esubject.htm.

———. Town of Canton (St. Lawrence County), 1870, 1880, 1900, 1910, 1920.

———. Town of Dannemora (Clinton County), 1880.

———. Town of De Kalb (St. Lawrence County), 1860, 1870.

———. Town of Potsdam (St. Lawrence County), 1870, 1880.

## Chapter 5

*Aluminum Bulletin* (Massena, NY). March 1918 to December 1920. Ogdensburg Public Library Archives. Newspaper Collection. Ogdensburg, NY. (Most articles are also available online from Northern New York Library Network, NYS Historic Newspapers. nyshistoricnewspapers.org.)

*Chicago Defender.* August 10, 1918; January 24, 1920; August 11, 1928; December 15, 1928. Ogdensburg Public Library Archives. Newspaper Collection. Ogdensburg, NY. (Most articles are also available online from Northern New York Library Network, NYS Historic Newspapers. nyshistoricnewspapers.org.)

*Commercial Advertiser* (Potsdam Junction, NY). October 9, 1917; January 20, 1925; March 19, 1929. Ogdensburg Public Library Archives. Newspaper Collection. Ogdensburg, NY. (Most articles are also available online from Northern New York Library Network, NYS Historic Newspapers. nyshistoricnewspapers.org.)

*Courier and Freeman.* October 10, 1917; October 19, 1921; May 20, 1925; June 24, 1925; September 15, 1926; June 22, 1927; September 18, 1928; June 26, 1929. Ogdensburg Public Library Archives. Newspaper Collection. Ogdensburg, NY. (Most articles are also available online from Northern New York Library Network, NYS Historic Newspapers. nyshistoricnewspapers.org.)

Danforth, R.T. Aluminum Company of America and Subsidiaries, Massena, NY. Chronological Notes. Massena Historical Association Archives, n.d.

Dupree, Mrs. Robert [Gloria McDonald Dupree]. Letter to Richard White, February 5, 1978. In possession of author.

Friedman, Saul S. *The Incident at Massena: The Blood Libel in America.* New York: Stein & Day Publishers, 1978.

*Gouverneur Free Press.* November 7, 1923; November 21, 1923; December 3, 1924; May 15, 1925; September 2, 1925; September 15, 1926; October 26, 1928. Ogdensburg Public Library Archives. Newspaper Collection. Ogdensburg, NY. (Most articles are also available online from Northern New York Library Network, NYS Historic Newspapers. nyshistoricnewspapers.org.)

*Hammond Advertiser.* December 6, 1924; May 28, 1925; June 25, 1925. Ogdensburg Public Library Archives. Newspaper Collection. Ogdensburg, NY. (Most articles are also available online from Northern New York Library Network, NYS Historic Newspapers. nyshistoricnewspapers.org.)

*Madrid Herald,* May 11, 1916. Ogdensburg Public Library Archives. Newspaper Collection. Ogdensburg, NY. (Most articles are also available online from Northern New York Library Network, NYS Historic Newspapers. nyshistoricnewspapers.org.)

*Massena Observer.* May 11, 1916; September 26, 1918; May 3, 1923; May 24, 1923; August 23, 1923; August 30, 1923; September 27, 1923; October 11, 1923; October 18, 1923; December 11, 1924; June 18, 1925; July 16, 1925; July 1, 1926; August 26, 1926; October 28, 1926; November 4, 1926; December 9, 1926; June 2, 1927; December 1, 1927; December 22, 1927; March 1, 1928; April 19, 1928; September 13, 1928. Ogdensburg Public Library Archives. Newspaper Collection. Ogdensburg, NY. (Most articles are also available online from Northern New York Library Network, NYS Historic Newspapers. nyshistoricnewspapers.org.)

*New York Times.* "Alien Labor Brought In." October 7, 1924.

———. "Aluminum Company Is Mellon Brothers Its President Says." October 8, 1924.

———. "Aluminum Strike Closes Six Plants; Picketing Orderly." August 12, 1934.

———. "Girl Mysteriously Slain." October 5, 1917.

———. "Massena Strike Settled." August 6, 1915.

———. "Mellon Visits Aluminum Plant." July 18, 1925.

———. "Militia Controls Massena." August 3, 1915.

———. "Militiamen Rout Mob at Massena." August 2, 1915.

———. "Pickets Busy at Massena." August 12, 1934.

———. "To Break Massena Strike: Aluminum Company Said to Be Gathering New Men for Factory." August 4, 1915.

*Northern Tribune* (Gouverneur, NY). February 17, 1915; September 8, 1926; September 5, 1928. Ogdensburg Public Library Archives. Newspaper Collection. Ogdensburg, NY. (Most articles are also available online from Northern New York Library Network, NYS Historic Newspapers. nyshistoricnewspapers.org.)

*Norwood News*. April 26, 1916; March 23, 1921; December 26, 1924. Ogdensburg Public Library Archives. Newspaper Collection. Ogdensburg, NY. (Most articles are also available online from Northern New York Library Network, NYS Historic Newspapers. nyshistoricnewspapers.org.)

*Ogdensburg Advance*. February 25, 1915; September 17, 1925; June 3, 1926; July 8, 1926; July 29, 1926; August 5, 1926; September 9, 1926; September 18, 1927; November 25, 1928; September 9, 1928; September 8, 1928. Ogdensburg Public Library Archives. Newspaper Collection. Ogdensburg, NY. (Most articles are also available online from Northern New York Library Network, NYS Historic Newspapers. nyshistoricnewspapers.org.)

*Ogdensburg Journal*. May 14, 1925. Ogdensburg Public Library Archives. Newspaper Collection. Ogdensburg, NY. (Most articles are also available online from Northern New York Library Network, NYS Historic Newspapers. nyshistoricnewspapers.org.)

*Potsdam Herald Recorder*. September 13, 1918; December 8, 1922; February 2, 1923; July 29, 1927. Ogdensburg Public Library Archives. Newspaper Collection. Ogdensburg, NY. (Most articles are also available online from Northern New York Library Network, NYS Historic Newspapers. nyshistoricnewspapers.org.)

*Republican Journal* (Ogdensburg, NY). October 5, 1917; October 11, 1917; October 13, 1917; October 14, 1920; June 4, 1921; October 13, 1921; January 18, 1922; March 28, 1922; August 18, 1922; October 16, 1922; October 24, 1922; December 7, 1922; January 25, 1923; May 1, 1923; September 21, 1923; December 11, 1923; July 14, 1924; August 20, 1924; October 4, 1924; January 9, 1925; May 2, 1925; May 18, 1925; May 20, 1925; June 26, 1925; September 5, 1925; September 16, 1925; September 9, 1926; September 17, 1926; September 17, 1928. Ogdensburg Public Library Archives. Newspaper Collection. Ogdensburg, NY. (Most articles are also available online from Northern New York Library Network, NYS Historic Newspapers. nyshistoricnewspapers.org.)

Stoller, Matt. *Goliath: The 100-Year War Between Monopoly Power and Democracy*. New York: Simon & Schuster, 2019.

United States Censuses, 1850, 1860, 1870, 1880, 1900, 1910, 1920, 1930. Washington, D.C.

U.S. Census Bureau. HeritageQuest Online, New York State Library, Databases and E-Journals. www.nysl.nysed.gov/gate/esubject.htm.

Virginia Commonwealth University Libraries. "Mapping the Second Ku Klux Klan, 1915–1940." N.d. labs.library.vcu.edu/klan.

White, Richard. Letter to the author, July 3, 2019. In possession of author.

# ABOUT THE AUTHOR

B ryan Thompson is a lifelong resident of St. Lawrence County. He holds a BS from Cornell University and an MS from SUNY Geneseo. He has published more than fifty articles on local history in local, regional and state publications. He was the 2009 winner of the New York State Archives and New York State Regents Bruce W. Dearstyne Award for excellence in educational use of historical records. He is also a recipient of a State Archives Hackman Research Fellowship.

An Association of Public Historians of New York State registered public historian, he is currently the municipal historian for the town of De Kalb.

*Visit us at*
www.historypress.com